MAGIC, MYTH, AND MONEY

MAGIC, MYTH, AND MONEY

The Origin of Money in Religious Ritual

WILLIAM H. DESMONDE

The Free Press of Glencoe, Inc.

A DIVISION OF THE CROWELL-COLLIER PUBLISHING COMPANY

For information, address:

The Free Press of Glencoe, Inc.
A DIVISION OF THE CROWELL-COLLIER PUBLISHING COMPANY
60 Fifth Avenue, New York 11

DESIGNED BY BERNARD SCHLEIFER

Library of Congress Catalog Card Number: 62-10584

Such was the vast power which the god settled in the lost island of Atlantis. . . . For many generations, as long as the divine nature lasted in them, they were obedient to the laws, and well-affectioned towards the god, whose seed they were; for they possessed true and in every way great spirits, uniting gentleness with wisdom in the various chances of life, and in their intercourse with one another. They despised everything but virtue, caring little for their present state of life, and thinking lightly of the possession of gold and other property, which seemed only a burden to them; neither were they intoxicated by luxury; nor did wealth deprive them of their self-control; but they were sober, and saw clearly that all these goods are increased by virtue and friendship with one another, whereas by too great regard and respect for them they are lost and friendship with them. By such reflections and by the continuance in them of a divine nature, the qualities which we have described grew and increased among them; but when the divine portion began to fade away, and became diluted too often and too much with the mortal admixture, and the human nature got the upper hand, they then, being unable to bear their fortune, behaved unseemly, and to him who had an eye to see, grew visibly debased, for they were losing the fairest of their precious gifts; but to those who had no eye to see the true happiness, they appeared glorious and blessed at the very time when they were full of avarice and unrighteous power.

—PLATO, *Critias*

PREFACE

Many of our economic institutions had their origin in practices which existed hundreds, even thousands of years ago, prior to the advent of science, the industrial revolution, and the urbanization of mankind. By understanding the ideas which generated these customs at their origin, we can more effectively affirm and revivify what is valuable in these traditions, and discard or restructure that which is destructive to the maturing of man's instinct for productive self-development.

Ancient Greek and Roman money originated as a religious symbol in sacrificial food communion rituals. Economic activity in antiquity, as Professor Karl Polanyi and others have emphasized, was embedded in the cultural institutions. Markets barely existed, and the production and distribution of goods was part of a system of kinship, magical, political, and religious relationships. Thus the original meaning of money in our culture was completely different from its modern significance as a medium of exchange or a unit of value in a market economy.

This essay is part of the author's larger interest in seeking to synthesize the insights of psychoanalysis with the findings of the social sciences and philosophy. The theory of interpersonal relations must be extended to include institutions such as money, which symbolizes reciprocal human relations on a national, indeed planetary scale. This book was originally planned as an exemplification of orthodox Freudian ideas. However, the author was increasingly drawn into problems, such as the origin of law, which he felt could not be adequately handled by Freud's main approach. Accordingly, the writer attempted to develop his own point of view, which is now eclectic. The Freudian influence is still present, but the sociological context of human relations stressed by Fromm has been emphasized. From Jung has come the conception that the mature person feels himself to be part of an ongoing religious tradition which gives his life meaning.

The author is not a psychoanalyst, but is primarily a social philosopher concerned with the perpetuation of humanity and the promotion of democracy, justice, and freedom. Hence, this book is to a large extent devoted to the psychology of the mature person and his civic interests and responsibilities. This orientation has led to discussions of human ideals, their relation to parental images, and their importance in cultural progress. The writer has taken the position that, just as an embryo cannot be properly comprehended without a knowledge of its potentialities as a mature organism, so a social group cannot be understood without a knowledge of its ideal form.

Some of the major philosophical influences in this book have been Whitehead's conception of creativity as the basic cosmic principle, and Josiah Royce's notion of individual fulfillment through loyal devotion. Extensive reference to material drawn from Frazer has been made, despite the fact that his writings are largely undiscussed by American anthropologists. The use of the comparative method in this book has been mainly for illustrative purposes, rather than for corroboration. Other writers whose work has played a prominent role are Fustel de Coulanges and Audrey I. Richards. The contributions of other theorists, such as Weber and Tawney, are implicit throughout the volume. The social psychology of George Herbert Mead, which is nowhere explicitly referred to, furnished the basic inspiration for this work, along with Harry Scherman's behavioristic analysis of economic activity, *The Promises Men Live By.*

The writer regards his viewpoints on religion as tentative and open for the development of further insight. Many important problems in theology, ethics, and political theory are touched upon in these pages, as well as controversial subjects in numerous special fields such as anthropology, numismatics, archaeology, and comparative law. In these instances, also, the points of view that have been taken should be regarded as subject to possible revision. The basic hypothesis of the origin of money in the ancient food communion rituals rests mainly upon the writings of Professor Bernhard Laum.

It is hoped that this book's study of early money symbolism will contribute to the theory of management and industrial sociology by helping to understand the motivations underlying modern man's quest for money. Although the institutional setting of contemporary money is far different from that of antiquity, it may be expected that many of the original motivations to some degree still exist. This may particularly be the case for the "organization man," who increasingly produces and consumes, not within a free market economy composed of a large number of small, independent enterprises, but within an economy composed of a handful of giant social structures which exert a powerful determining influence upon his emotional life, personal development, and integrity.

A number of people have very kindly read all or parts of the manuscript, and have given me the benefit of their criticism, both positive and negative. These individuals include Leonard Feldstein, Siegfried Garbuny, Sol Posensky, George Devereux, Theodor Frankel, I. P. Glauber, Kurt Goldstein, Samuel R. Lehrman, Karl Menninger, and Meyer Schapiro. I am grateful to Joseph Campbell and Karl Polanyi for their encouragement. Some of the above individuals have disagreed with me on important points, but I thank them all for their interest and help. Arthur Liebers has made many useful editorial suggestions. My wife has assisted me in the research, planning, and writing of this book, as well as in the numerous clerical activities involved in the preparation of the manuscript.

WILLIAM H. DESMONDE

September, 1961

CONTENTS

» *xi*

Part Two

Religious and Parental Images
in Ancient City Life

Part Three
Kinship Feelings in Fertility Rituals

Part Four
The Origin of Money
in the Sacrificial Meal

Part Five
Money in the Holy Community

Part Six
Further Speculations on
the Significance of Ancient Money

PART I

From Holy Communion
to Hard Cash

one

MODERN MAN
IN SEARCH OF
HIS MONEY

1. THE MYSTERY OF MONEY

Few institutions have as pervasive an influence as money upon every man's opportunity to give himself to others in love and work. The fulfillment of our emotional and intellectual potentialities is to a large extent influenced by the functioning of money in human relations.

Yet, to many of us, money is a mystery, a symbol handled mainly by the priests of high finance, and regarded by us with much of the same reverence and awe as the primitive feels to-

ward the sacred relics providing magical potency in a tribal ritual.
As if in a higher plane of reality, the symbol seems to operate in
an incomprehensible, mystical way, understood and controllable
only by the magic of brokers, accountants, lawyers, and financiers.
Listen to the litany of the business page:

> The new $1.50 preferred stock will be junior to the $1.25
> preferred stock and will have a liquidating and call price of $25
> a share. This stock will be serviced by a sinking fund into which
> the corporation will make an initial payment of four per cent,
> or $137,578, of the aggregate call price of the stock on June 1,
> and one per cent of the aggregate call price quarterly thereafter.

Like spellbound savages in the presence of the holy, we
watch in wonder the solemn proceedings, feeling in a vague,
somewhat fearful way that our lives and the happiness of our
children are at the mercy of mysterious forces beyond our control. The eerie music and the strange chants continue:

> Cotton futures moved ten points off to four points up yester-
> day in moderate trading. The market opened steady, one to
> seven points higher. Early in the session there was some buying
> by foreign brokers and some trade support, but hedge selling
> and liquidation increased later. A sale of 10,000 bales of Decem-
> ber, and 1,000 bales of July was made by a large commission
> house. Liverpool futures closed five to seven English points lower.

Apart from the esoteric rites of high finance, money seems to
function in everyday life much like a miraculous talisman, bringing to us the gratification of almost every conceivable desire.
Wherever we go, if we have money, people hasten to do our
bidding, as if placed under a magical charm by the presence
of these worn-down coins and soiled pieces of green paper. The
vast profusion of goods which are offered in the shops of the
big city are ours to possess, if we have money. Every imaginable
luxury is available for purchase, and if these goods are not exactly what we want, hundreds and thousands of craftsmen and
manufacturers are eager to gratify our special needs or whims.
Not only does money buy goods, but it buys the services of

people—their time, toil, and ingenuity. Men will pilot planes, go under the sea, burrow in the ground, they will go to the ends of the earth, through deserts, mountains, and icy wastes —for money. They will pay deference, flatter, be grateful, hurry or wait, teach or learn. For money, humans can be found to furnish love or to commit murder.

Like a magical charm, money brings power, which can be used either for good or bad purposes. Hospitals can be built, universities endowed, slums cleared, lives enriched. But with the same power high officials can be moved, political influence connived, honest men ruined financially and morally, and people twisted and hurt in a multitude of ways. So varied and enormous are the uses of money that it can almost be thought to provide us with a type of omnipotence. Even immortality can be attempted through the astute use of advertising and publicity.

Certainly money has a powerful effect upon our inner feelings of anxiety, and to a large extent our quest for this symbol is motivated by the desire to find something akin to a magical charm for attaining emotional security in a world of turmoil and sudden change. We might conjecture that gambling is an atavistic desire to attain miraculously a source of security and omnipotence without the hard work and renunciation necessary for earning a living.

Psychoanalytic theory suggests that for many people money is a symbol of an unconscious infantile desire to attain a union in absolute dependency upon the father and mother. At the same time, however, money also symbolizes the ambivalence of the child toward its parents. The desire to possess the mother and to destroy the father rival seems to be indicated in the ruthless, compulsive quest for money exhibited by many people. Such financial terms as bank "panic," corporate "securities," or government "bond" suggest the emotional background of money; and the reckless enthusiasm of the business boom and the riotous spending of money on credit offer promising fields for the application of psychoanalytic theory to mass psychology.

Even in everyday life, money acts as if it possesses a mystical virtue for bringing together all men into a unity of physical and emotional interdependence. Through money, the forces of supply and demand, however separate by distance or custom, intimately and reciprocally bind almost everyone on earth into a community of hopes, fears, dreams, hostilities, and loves.

Stripped, however, of their glamour, magic, and incomprehensibility, the most complex monetary symbolisms stand revealed to us merely as institutions which through centuries have developed out of the quest of human beings for self-fulfillment. For money, in all of its varied, mysterious, and abstract forms, is our own creation, and has no meaning apart from the needs and desires of men. Psychoanalysts speak, with great insight, of the necessity of loving others and of the determination of our emotional and intellectual life by powerful unconscious symbols; but it is largely within the sociological matrix furnished by monetary practices that we have the opportunity to actualize our potentialities. Indeed, of all of the great symbols which have arisen out of history to shape the consciousness of man, few have had such a powerful, direct influence upon our personality growth and our human relations.

In a legal sense, the value of money is based ultimately upon large quantities of gold and silver which have with great difficulty and expense been dug out of the ground in different parts of the world, refined, cast into ingots, then buried in the ground again, in the vaults of various governments. Paradoxically, it is illegal for the average man to possess the gold which is supposedly the basis for the value of his money.

These oddities emphasize the fact that money is in actuality a symbol of the emotional relations between an individual and the other members of his group. It is a representation, and an emergent from the cooperative activities of a number of individuals, manifested in expectations and hopes on one side, and by a sense of obligation and appreciation on the other. Money is the record of a complex emotional system comprised of the rights and correlative promises arising out of human actions in the past and human faith in the future.[1]

Society is based to a large extent upon these promises; the word "credit" literally means "faith." It is the expansion and contraction of this "faith" which creates many of the most mystifying aspects of money. To a large extent, money has become a record of interpersonal promises. For example, most of us work at our jobs for several days or weeks, receiving in return only a "paycheck," which is a company's promise to pay, based in turn on a bank's promise to pay. We deposit the check, and issue promises to pay—our personal checks—to the butcher, landlord, and doctor, who in turn deposit these promises in their bank, which is very likely the same as our own. What has actually happened? A large number of bookkeeping changes have taken place, but no cash has been exchanged. The fact is that over ninety percent of all commercial transactions are carried on by checks, and a large part of the money in existence, such as savings accounts, bonds, and insurance policies, exists merely in the form of records in the offices of various big companies.

With the advent of electronic memories and computers, the handling of money is being taken over by magnetized spots or electrical impulses within data-processing machines which keep record of interpersonal expectations and promises. The technology of high-speed mathematical-logical decision-making can be expected to introduce increasing rationality into human relations. But regardless of the form it takes, the symbol of money can be regarded as a type of seal of good faith, marking society's indebtedness to an individual for his services to the community.

2. THE ANTHROPOLOGICAL APPROACH TO ECONOMICS

Most of the theories of the economists neglect the psychological, cultural, and historical setting of monetary symbols. For many economists, money is related only to the equilibrium of the forces of supply and demand, operating under whatever constraints may be present in the market. Mention a few of the concepts used by economists and financiers: "fixed and variable agents of production," "marginal productivity and imputation," "rediscount rate and fluctuations in the money market," "liquidity preference," "noncumulative preferred stock," "commodity futures." These terms pertain to matters of the utmost importance, but to be understood fully these concepts must not be regarded as the cold data of "the economic system," abstracted out of the emotional matrix in which people live and work. For supply and demand and the intricacies of the monetary system are basically nothing but human struggles, sacrifices, and joys; these are the realities underlying economic activity.

Anthropology reveals clearly this matrix of human motivations upon which economic behavior rests in other societies. The school of "institutional economics" has adopted this approach, and has stressed the fact that human values generate the culture pattern within which the forces of supply and demand operate. The forms of our particular economic institutions are not inherent in man's nature, for many other societies have different methods for organizing human work and mutual aid. The shapes and forms of money depend upon the human motivations expressed in the social institutions of each culture. For example, the production and exchange of goods very often exists in the complete absence of a barter or market pattern. Ours is the only society in which an all-encompassing market system has evolved. In no other civilization has the market ever come to have such a pervasive and penetrating linkage to so many aspects of human life.[2]

3. THE IDEALS OF MONEY

One practice commonly known to us from anthropology is the custom of the potlatch, the use of economic interchange for the ostentatious display and conspicuous consumption of wealth. Similar motivations often underlie the use of money in our culture. In this respect, money functions as a type of medal, which enables us to "show off" to others, and to make them envious.

Money frequently serves as a means of compensating for our inner feelings of inferiority, and for enabling us to revenge ourselves upon others who have slighted us. In a rawer form, there is often a conscious desire to humiliate the other, to "make him eat his heart out" by getting him to feel that he has been completely unsuccessful in life compared to ourselves. Whipped on by the scorn and condescension of others, we ceaselessly strive "to show them all," by "rubbing it in" through a display of our wealth. These attitudes can often be observed in the rivalry among children for the love and approval of their parents, and no doubt these motivations are frequently carried over into their struggle for money in adult life.

For many of us, the full actualization of our potentialities means becoming a financial success; so that in this respect money serves as a medal of life achievement. The amassing of money is for a great number of individuals their main aim, and the mark of a life well spent. Not to acquire a large sum of money is to be a failure.

But being a financial success is often a poor indication of a person's value to society, for there are many ways in which people can make or lose money which have little to do with their merits and their contributions to society. The shrewd cheat prospers and the hardworking innocent is led to financial slaughter. Fortunes are founded on crimes and corrupt practices, dishonest individuals prosper through shady deals, and slick operators earn a fat living from maneuverings which raise them high above their merited station. Many professions are under-paid, and some occupations furnish excessive compensation. Sometimes the sincere contributor to the welfare of society is unappreciated and neglected. In such ways, our monetary institutions frequently fail to reward people for their true service to the community.

For those individuals who love their work and feel that it is meaningful, productive efforts are a type of devotion, a cooperative effort and renunciation carried on with enjoyment and self-fulfillment. Such an emotion is felt by an artist who pours his heart into his creation. The notion of work as devotion has largely vanished for large numbers of people in the modern world. The production of goods in the Middle Ages by craftsmen was truly a vocation, a task to which they felt called. Something of this feeling probably exists in primitive societies, in which production, distribution, and consumption is usually carried on as an exchange of gifts among members of the same kinship group. The saying, "Blessed is he who has found his work" illustrates a conception of work as a joyful sacrifice, as a form of true love.

Ideally, money can be said to symbolize the devotion and gratitude among a group of friends working together for the good of the community. In a utopia, the seller and the buyer would be dedicated friends exchanging tokens of love.

The basic yearning of our emotional life is for freely given devotion to the advancement of human welfare, freely given because we feel ourselves most fulfilled when we are able to pour our hearts into a mutual sharing with the past, present, and future members of history. The fulfillment of this basic emotional need may be regarded as the true function of money—a giving and receiving springing from our innermost self out of a deep sense of joy and abundance.

This quest for unity is the oldest of mankind's aspirations, for it is the deepest of all our yearnings. Money in this respect is the longing for true love.

Although money has failed to achieve this unity, all of us feel this sense of oneness occasionally, as for example when we perform a charitable act, or when, like primitive people, we exchange gifts among our kinship group. It is at times such as Christmas that we most keenly feel this inner spirit of emotional fulfillment. When we buy presents during this holiday period, we feel a sense of joyousness in purchasing what we wish to give to the other. The pleasure of the giver lies in the pleasure that the receiver will experience from the gift. Even the canned sentimentality of the advertisements fails to destroy our sense of uplift during the Christmas season.

The thought of money as symbolizing the Christmas spirit at first strikes us as completely unreal and discordant. We are accustomed to thinking of money as "the root of all evil," in terms of "hard cash" and the "dog eat dog" competitive struggle within the business world. How, then, can we say that the true function of money is to symbolize a spirit of love linking all men? Possibily the reason for our surprise and inability to comprehend this equation of money and universal friendship is because many of us have tended to become crusty and calloused, while inwardly we are kind and warm, yearning to give and take in a spirit of inner abundance and freedom.

4. NEUROSIS AND ALIENATION FROM WORK

Indeed, many of the neuroses of contemporary times may well originate from our loss of the feeling that life has meaning, that we belong to a history made possible by the efforts and sacrifices of our predecessors. Modern man rarely feels that his devoted work contributes to a tradition of human progress. He is often alienated from what he produces, and in this way misses a necessary emotional satisfaction.

Lacking this sense of meaningfulness in our lives, we seek other gratifications, which, since they do not answer to our deeper needs, cause us aimlessly to pursue superficial interests. The frustration of our instinct for higher fulfillment results in neurosis.

Our attitude toward money symbolizes this neurosis, for money is a means of communication between an individual and his society, but this form of communication no longer provides communion. Modern money exemplifies contemporary man's lack of unity with his civilization and its goals, for although money has become an institution which brings together almost everyone into an international division of labor and consumption, it has not created friendship or genuine regard among men. People struggle for more and more money, and are unaware that the proper function of this institution is to facilitate mutual self-actualization in economic relations.

In fact, a recent important contribution to economic thought, the theory of strategy,[3] is completely unconcerned with the role of money in love, justice, and interpersonal fulfillment. This theory regards economic behavior as a game in which success is largely a matter of making convenient coalitions with others, at the same time manipulating them through pretension and bluff. The market is seen as similar to a poker game, in which there is no warm, appreciative consideration of what each participant deserves for his merits and devoted work, but rather a cold, shrewd calculation of how to take advantage of everyone else with the maximum efficiency. This is the attitude of the trader, who bargains not with the aim of determining what society owes a person for his work, but of exploiting other individuals by playing upon their anxieties, credulity, and lack of information.

Far from being society's medal of heroism to outstanding citizens, money becomes, insofar as the theory of strategy is applicable, simply a means for facilitating the payoff in an institution operating like a poker game. Love, devotion to work, and the maximum actualization of every man's potentialities play little part in the activities of the trader in the marketplace. A sincere person can only with great difficulty attain self-realization in a bargaining situation requiring the wily distortion or withholding of information for selfish purposes. The meaning of sacrifice for the promotion of the general welfare is completely lost in this type of group psychology, and money tends to become a symbol of a rough, fierce, and unremitting struggle for survival. Certain of the views of Freud could be interpreted as the reaction of a sensitive person striving to adjust himself to this type of situation:

> Not merely is this stranger on the whole not worthy of love, but, to be honest, I must confess he has more claim to my hostility, even to my hatred. He does not seem to have the least

trace of love for me, does not show me the slightest consideration. If it will do him any good, he has no hesitation in injuring
me, never even asking himself whether the amount of advantage
he gains by it bears any proportion to the amount of wrong done
to me.[4]

The prevalence of slick deception and manipulation in modern economic life, which prevents men from pouring their hearts
into loyal devotion to industrial activities, has caused many individuals to lose sight of, or despair of attaining the ideal of
living together with a group of genuine, appreciative people.
In such circumstances, hedonism, the symptom of a diseased
society in which individuals are unable to find lasting satisfaction and fulfillment in their work, tends to enter psychological,
sociological, and political theory, undermining the social scientist's true function of moral leadership. The feeling of futility
increases, the culture loses its vigor, and people sink into boredom, callousness, and the quest for superficial pleasure. As
T.S. Eliot describes "The Wasteland":

> What are the roots that clutch, what branches grow
> Out of this stony rubbish? Son of man,
> You cannot say, or guess, for you know only
> A heap of broken images, where the sun beats,
> And the dead tree gives no shelter, the cricket no relief,
> And the dry stone no sound of water . . .*

It may well be that in many spheres of modern life man is
approaching a state of emotional bankruptcy. For our most vital
capital, as some of our greatest industrialists have recognized, is
not in our existent factories and inventories, but is in the creative
enthusiasm which within the last few hundred years has enabled
man to transform the physical world around him, and which,
provided the institution of money is properly understood, will
enable him ultimately to conquer the universe.

---

* From "The Waste Land," in *Collected Poems 1909-1935* by T. S.
Eliot, copyright, 1936, by Harcourt, Brace & World, Inc. Reprinted by
permission of Harcourt, Brace & World, Inc., and of Faber and Faber Ltd.

two

MONEY AND
THE QUEST FOR
THE HOLY GRAIL

1. MONEY AND HUMAN NEEDS

What is money? Anthropology shows that almost every object we can conceive of has in one culture or another been used as money. Whales' teeth, feathers, beads, rice, drums, gongs, cannon, bees' wax, tea, salt, cocoa, and reindeer are among the vast variety of things which have been employed for this purpose. We ourselves are accustomed to thinking of money in modern terms, but the nature of this symbol has undergone many changes in the course of history. Not long ago in the United

States the use of silver as money was a controversial subject; and the last century has witnessed an evolution from coinage to greenbacks, and finally a partial transformation to holes in punched cards and polarized spots on magnetic tapes.

Whatever symbolic form it may take, money is in actuality a social institution devised to regulate the numerous emotions involved in the giving and taking activities of cooperating people. The story of money is therefore a study in the entire range of human motivation, from the heights of heroism to the depths of infantilism and greed. It is a study in love and hate, enthusiasm and guilt, ambition and renunciation, maturity and ignorance, and communion and conflict. Underlying all of these motivations, however, we may discern one basic drive—the quest for self-actualization. And to attain this fulfillment of his potentialities, each man must enter into productive, loving relationships with others.

Regardless, therefore, of the symbols in which it is expressed and the purposes it may serve at any particular time or place, the proper, ideal function of money is to provide an institutional framework within which all men can actualize their potentialities through the establishment of creative human relations. Strictly speaking, money is not a symbol at all, but is the ideal of dedicated sharing within the division of labor in society. We will conceive of money as an ideal, even though, as we shall also seek to demonstrate, money is also symbolic of man's atavistic desire for omnipotence—a motivation which often overshadows, if not obliterates, the higher goals for which this institution strives. The wish to share the joy of mutual devotion is the deepest of all desires, and money can therefore be regarded as a quest, a search for emotional unity in group psychology which persists even in the face of injustice and evil. This longing for true love is basic within the heart of every man, and the history of money is the story of the forms which this yearning has taken.

These are our contentions, and to prove them we shall go back through the centuries to the origins of money in ancient

Greece and Rome. We shall encounter many strange practices and beliefs in the course of this emotional history, many of which will seem to lead us far afield from the subject of money; but we will ultimately show how these early customs and ideas gave rise to the monetary symbol as we now know it.

2. THE ROOTS OF MONEY

The emotional roots of money lie deep in the past, in traditions which have developed over the millennia. Experiences of strong intensity leave a lasting impression upon the hearts and minds of men, causing them to form the religious, sociological, and psychological beliefs which inspire the institutions governing human relations. Through conscious or unconscious modes of communication, these depth experiences are passed down through the centuries, perpetuating what are felt to be fundamental truths about man's destiny in the cosmos and how he should live with his fellow men. We cannot properly understand the modern United States, for example, without having a grasp of the traditions resulting from the Civil War, the Declaration of Independence, the Magna Charta, or the Protestant Reformation.

The breakdown of traditional beliefs may be either harmful or beneficial. Great insights reached in ancient times, leading to the formation of basic social institutions, such as money, may be lost, the surviving symbols remaining as meaningless decorations to the people of the present, whereas to the past these symbols may have expressed the essence of reality. On the other hand, ancient beliefs, conceived in the days of man's ignorance and superstition, may be perpetuated in our contemporary institutions, serving only to stultify man's present efforts, and to perpetuate emotions and ideas which are detrimental to his present growth.

The study of the origin of human institutions and their sur-

vival as important determinants of modern man's self-fulfillment
enables us to assess more adequately their present value for
human betterment. Such an investigation can perhaps help us
to regain insight into dynamisms which, in an unconscious way,
underlie our modern practices in interpersonal relations. The
loss of an insight which may have provided a basic driving
force behind our culture can possibly lead to drift and despair,
neurosis and destruction, unless the vision is revitalized.

T. S. Eliot's "The Wasteland" may be said to express the feeling of hollowness symbolized by modern money, resulting from
the absence in our civilization of a set of cultural goals and
purposes which impart enthusiasm to life, love, and work.

This poem was to a great extent based upon the myth of the
quest for the Holy Grail. Many of the great beliefs of mankind
are expressed in the legends, mythology, and literature of the
past; and from these sources we can glimpse the powerful emotional symbols upon which our civilization is founded. One of
the most important traditions in the western world is exemplified
in the tales of chivalry, the story of King Arthur and the Knights
of the Round Table. The heroic ideals of courage, comradely
loyalty, and religious devotion are expressed in these legends of
the pure knight venturing forth and enduring innumerable
hazards and dangers in quest of the Holy Grail.

The ideal of the English gentleman stems from the knightly
tradition expressed in the Grail legends, and it is no coincidence
that a writer such as Tennyson chose the Arthurian mythology to
exalt a majestic, if somewhat narrow, conception of British greatness.

The American way of life is deeply imbued with the English
tradition, and our desire to emulate this aristocratic ideal provides much of our incentive for obtaining money. The manners,
decorum, and bearing of the British gentleman provide a model
for identification, and the goal of economic life for many people
is to identifiy with this nobility. Critics such as Veblen have
penetratingly debunked this aspiration (which was particularly
evident in the nineteenth century) to emulate the snobbery,
parasitism, and exploitativeness of the English leisure class; but

the ideals of clean manliness and gallantry toward enemies remain among our highest standards of personal conduct. So that the desire for money, insofar as it is based on the wish to be identified with the British gentleman, reflects not only the vain incentives of conspicuous leisure and ostentatious display, but also genuine goals of character development. In an ideal sense, then, the quest for money is identical with the search for the Holy Grail.

The knightly ideal is of course not limited to the English, and it would be a gross omission to ignore the valuable traditions from many other sources which are present in the American way of life. In fact, the ideas expressed in the Holy Grail legends form part of the cultural heritage of Europe, if not of the entire civilized world.

Scholars have devoted much energy to the study of the origins of the Arthurian legends. It has been suggested that these tales did not originate simply in the imagination of poets, but stemmed from ancient sacramental communion rituals presided over by a priestly king, in which the participants ate a common meal to symbolize their feelings of mutual devotion and fellowship. The Holy Grail, according to this viewpoint, was in its origin the food which symbolized the bonds of loyalty among the communicants. The story of King Arthur and the Knights of the Round Table is analogous to the Last Supper, the Holy Grail being the vessel used when Christ ate the Paschal Lamb with his disciples. One school of thought holds that the Holy Grail legend goes back in history beyond the Christian eucharist, to pagan rites[1] which preceded the emergence of Christianity by thousands of years, and which represented one of man's earliest efforts to establish a world religion based on universal fellowship.[*] Thus the cultural goals from which modern man obtains his incentives for acquiring money extend back to the remotest eras in the history of civilization.

A persistent motif in the Arthurian legends is the presence

---

[*] Other scholars, however, regard the Arthurian legends as originating principally in Celtic mythology. For example Roger Sherman Loomis', *Arthurian Tradition and Chrétien de Troyes.*[2]

of a blight upon the land, resulting from the weakening of the vitality of the king, which can be restored only by the finding of the Holy Grail. The knight's quest for the sacred vessel is actually a type of initiation, in which the seeker's task is to find the source of grace and energy which is lacking both in the country and within himself.

Modern sociology and religious thought provides an explanation of the real meaning of these myths; the lack of a feeling of belonging, and the absence of social cohesion and higher dedication were the true blights upon the land. Only by reestablishing feelings of genuine friendship and emotional commitment could the sense of futility and meaninglessness be removed from the society. So that the knight's quest for the Holy Grail, which kept appearing and disappearing miraculously in all manner of strange places, was really a search for emotional warmth and fellowship.

Today man is becoming increasingly aware of the emptiness in his life, and he yearns to find something which will fill him again with a zest for living. Many individuals seek to find a feeling of grace, or wholeness, through the acquisition of more and more money. We all seem to be searching for the Holy Grail, but in vain, for the holy relic seems to have vanished from the land. Sociologically speaking, it could be said that we have lost sight of the true meaning of money—the expression of loyalty in economic relations. The story of money, like the myth of the Holy Grail, is a tale of the corruption of ancient ideals of virtue by slowly corroding evil.

The institution of money and the myth of the Holy Grail have deep affinities, both in meaning and in historical origin. Both express a yearning which has motivated men throughout the centuries—a longing for a world society based on love among all people. This book is a history of that quest, a search which began in the earliest epochs of the Graeco-Roman civilization. The first form of money was shared food, which for many centuries preceded the evolution of coinage. Coinage, we shall see, had the same significance as the Grail—that of a sacred relic symbolizing a holy meal among a loyal fellowship. For research has demonstrated that money, in our culture, originated in an identical manner as the Holy Grail, in a ritual communion meal in which the shared food symbolized mutual dedication among the communicants. Our money began as a religious symbol in early Greek and Roman society.

3. THE NATURE OF RELIGION

What is a religious symbol? Before we can discuss the historical origin of money, we must comprehend the meaning of numerous religious practices. Our plan is to devote the first half of this book to these preparatory explanations. We will first consider how ideal aspirations entered into the symbolism of early money, and will then discuss the everyday brutal realities of human ambivalence and conflict which suffused the economic activities of ancient men.

Ethical values are a necessary condition for a mature emotional life, and amidst the force, fear, and hate which have always played an important, often decisive part in social affairs, the human soul—the need to give and receive love—has frequently been a major factor in the formation of man's early institutions. In the preliminary chapters of this book, we shall not be concerned so much with the realities of ancient life as with the higher aspirations represented in rites and symbols. Insofar as man's ethical ideals are concerned, and however barbaric and cruel the reality may have been,[3] economic relations in ancient times were to some extent conceived of as religious relations. To the degree that these religious ideas were rational, economic activities expressed one of the deepest of man's longings—his desire to enter fully into a shared life with others. In this lofty sense, despite the slavery, oppression, and warfare which existed in early Greece and Rome, money symbolized the loving giving and taking among individuals which gave men the feeling of having emotional roots in their community. The community was a religious congregation, and all members felt themselves to be fellows in a sacred communion. In theory at least, these beliefs were thought to enrich life, and to give the culture its vitality.

We do not assert that many people practiced these beliefs, or even that these ideals were formulated in the early times, before philosophers such as Plato; but we do contend that these ethical aspirations were latent within the minds of men, just as the capacity to walk is latent within the psyche of the crawling baby. So that the absence of these ideals in the minds and actions of the ancients does not prove that these capacities for mature, civilized life were not present at the core. The fact is that for early men, as for the modern infant, the first beginnings of higher cultural activity were expressed in the grosser bodily needs. Money, as we have said, originated in what is perhaps the most elementary activity of all—eating.

4. FOOD, MONEY, AND THE DIVINE POWERS

It is not too astonishing to find that money in our culture originated in the eating of food, for one of the most frequent and forceful ways in which money enters our lives is through its use in satisfying hunger. We must eat, and we are dependent upon others for food through a complex organization of commercial institutions which link the big cities to the farms. The human organism must maintain its metabolism through eating, and we eat by giving money to those with whom we are interdependent.

The institution of money establishes an intimate linkage between our external environment and our internal organs. Our physiology, and hence our emotional life and drive to live, is bound up with our monetary relations with other people. The quantity of sugar in our blood stream, the tonus of the muscles in our alimentary tract, and our blood pressure are part of the same causal nexus as the velocity of demand deposits, the short interest at the Stock Exchange, and the stability of the English pound.

Money enters into our lives as a powerful symbol dominating a large part of our conscious and unconscious activities, and human conceptions of food, the basic economic commodity, are the prototype of attitudes toward the functioning of the money institution. The early history of money is largely the history of the meaning of food for early man. Indeed, the common meal was the first money in our culture, and this shared food, or love feast, was at the core of the social institutions of Greek and Roman antiquity.

In ancient times, men lived in small kinship groups, very similar to those constituting the primitive societies studied by modern anthropologists. Under these crude conditions, the threat of hunger is of daily concern to everyone, and the obtaining and distribution of food occupies a large proportion of each person's work and conscious activities. Both in the economists' sense of the term, and in the ethical philosophers' usage, food is the *good* of the community. The anthropologist Audrey I. Richards has dwelt upon the emotional significance of food in the life of primitive cultures:

> In most savage tribes starvation is a constant possibility, if not an actual menace. The food quest is the chief occupation of every active member of the community, and their most important institutions are concerned with the ownership and distribution of supplies. The emotional life of the primitive man is, therefore, chiefly dominated by his nutritive desires and anxieties. . . .[4]

The eating of food is an experience felt more keenly after prolonged hunger, or when limited nourishment is obtained only after great hardship and danger. Under these primitive circumstances, food not only provides an immediate physical pleasure, but also gives the individual a pronounced inner feeling of increasing strength and bodily replenishment. He feels life with added intensity, with *gusto*. This surge of power, growth, and renewed creativity within primitive man contributes, through empathy, to his experience of the existence of similar powers and vitalities in the world around him. These feelings, no doubt often of a gross and material nature, contribute to early man's religious world-view, in which all objects in the outer world, such as rocks, trees, springs, and stars, are believed to be vital, holy personalities. Primitive man exists in a kinship relationship to the cosmos,[5] feeling himself personally involved with the wills populating the external environment.

The trend of civilized thought for centuries has been the gradual depersonalization of the universe, and only occasionally, as in the poet's device of "personification," do we find traces of this once prevalent conception. Yet modern biology, in a very scientific, sophisticated way, appears to be rediscovering a feeling for man as having a destiny in a universe composed of vital forces.[6] The phenomenon of organic life, according to a growing number of contemporary scientists, represents a cosmic force that lifts energy to higher levels of order. From this standpoint, man, as an organism representing the manifestation in nature of the organization of energy, is a triumphant expression of the creative force in the universe.[7] The growth of culture represents the victory of the life force over the principle of disintegration, the conquest of disorder by order. Freud's conception of the death instinct may be equated with the continual degradation of the energy in the universe to lower levels, while Love, or Eros, may be identified with the growth of culture and rationality.

The eating of food in common therefore represented to ancient man the sharing of a vital power, participation in a mutual source of strength. This is the root significance of both money and the Holy Grail—a symbol, or vessel, containing a holy vitality, to be shared among a group of individuals dedicated to the advancement of love, creativity, and order.

The constant menace of starvation in a primitive society threatens the very existence of the community, and it is under such circumstances that the basic values in human relations are felt most deeply. The successful facing of such a danger requires the full commitment of each individual to the welfare of the group. The human "soul" may be defined as a person's dedication to the continuation and promotion of human welfare under a condition of crisis.

The hero in a primitive community is frequently the person most proficient in obtaining nutrition. Success in the quest for food, Richards states, "determines almost universally social prestige in a savage society . . . Such success may depend either on individual qualities—endurance, daring, and patient concentration—or the attainment of special skill and facility."[8] The true worth of an individual is often discerned under such conditions of peril; and it is sometimes only under such circumstances that a person discovers his soul, becoming able to separate superficial strivings from deeper fulfillments.

A religious experience is valid when a person feels within himself a creative force driving him to make a full emotional commitment to strive for the survival of the community. The strength of character developed when an individual meets a challenge to his self-actualization imbues him with a deep source of inner power for facing the future with confidence and with success. The religious experience is thus the emotional enrichment resulting from an individual's identification with the creative forces of nature, in the face of a dangerous situation representing a disintegrative power. A main function of religious rite is the revivification and perpetuation of this productive dedication, upon which, as Toynbee states, the growth of civilization depends.

For ancient man, the sharing of food was a sacred ritual, in which the participants renewed their creative commitment by re-identifying themselves with a common source of strength and energy. The obtaining of food under conditions of peril was for these early men an expression of heroism and honor; and, as in the story of King Arthur and the Knights of the Round Table, only those who had proved themselves in these traits of character were accepted as members of the communion. Participation in the shared food was therefore equivalent to receiving a medal for courage and devotion. Money originated as a symbol of man's soul.

PART 2

Religious and Parental Images
in Ancient City Life

three

THE FAMILY MEAL

1. KINSHIP FEELINGS

The first form which was taken by money was simply the family meal, and the ideals embodied in this common repast of the kinfolk became one of the great traditions of our civilization.

Who does not remember with nostalgia the family dinner, where in the midst of cherished, *familiar* people and objects, all partook of Mother's cooking? In ruder times, the entire family ate from a common bowl, and this food-containing vessel symbolized the deep sentimental ties among all of the members of the kinship group.

The earliest societies were composed of kinfolk, and it was within these groups that individuals first felt themselves to be a part of a continuity of community life. Identification with the traditions of the family, embodied by the common meal, gave the individual a feeling of warmth, vitality, and inspiration. In the ancient Graeco-Roman civilization, the first social groups were simply enlargements of the patriarchal family, either by legal fiction (ritual adoption) or by birth. These early communities took the form of what the German sociologist Tönnies called the *Gemeinschaft*, or folk society:

> The people see themselves surrounded by the inhabited earth. It seems as if, in the beginning of time, the earth itself had brought from its womb the human beings who look upon her as their mother . . . The area settled and occupied is therefore a common heritage, the land of the ancestors toward which all feel and act as descendants and blood brothers. . . . It represents a common sphere of will and not only upholds the unity of contemporaneous generations but also links together past and future ones. Habit, next to ties of blood, forms the strongest bond among contemporaries, and, likewise, memory links the living to the dead. The homeland, as the embodiment of dear memories, holds the heart of man, who parts from it with sorrow and from abroad looks back to it with homesickness and longing. As the place where ancestors lived and died, where their spirits will dwell and command the thoughts of the living, it acquires for simple and pious minds and hearts enhanced and sublime significance.[1]

2. WORK AND TRADITION IN THE FOLK SOCIETY

The development of some type of monetary institution to facilitate the division of labor and consumption is a necessary condition for the emergence of the city from the folk society, and the spiritual rootlessness of the modern city-dweller goes hand in hand with the decay of the ancient ideals which originally gave rise to money. We cannot comprehend the emotional significance of money without understanding the ideals from which it sprang. There is a natural tendency, of course, for the modern urbanite, disillusioned by the impersonality, unfriendliness, and callousness of life in the big city, to romanticize about the folk society, forgetting its stubborn backwardness, fixed social hierarchies, its ignorance, vulgarity, and cruelty. Without falling into this error, however, we plan to devote the next few chapters to the sentimental aspects of the simple kinship community, for these are as much of a reality as the raw barbarisms which we shall discuss later in the book.

From this sentimental standpoint, then, we may say that the member of the folk society felt his work to be part of a great chain of efforts made by the dead, the living, and those not yet born. His soul was expressed by his identification with the past, present, and future members of the community. This person received inspiration from feeling himself to be a significant part of history, a segment of a great community process which had its roots in the remote past, and which was aimed toward higher achievements in times to come.

The family meal enabled the member of the kinship group to feel that his life had meaning. Loneliness, the emotion of futility, and ennui did not play an important part in his life, as the division of labor, in which his energies were absorbed, was the expression of mutual love. He possessed creative vigor and vitality, for his identification with his work provided fulfillment for his deepest desires. Some of this spirit survives in our modern home life, but it is doubtful if the same feeling of rootedness in the land and in history is present in the kitchenettes and dining foyers of the transient population of the city apartment and the suburban housing development.

Dedication to the advance of culture is a manifestation of the vital forces in nature, and the fullest meaning of life is derived from the individual's commitment to such a tradition. In working to achieve human progress, a person is able to feel that he has not lived in vain, that in some way his efforts are embodied in future social life. For tradition includes, as a necessary component, a respect and appreciation for those who have lived in the past, and whose lives have made the present social group possible. In contributing to the family meal, the ancient individual felt a responsibility to the future members of the community, for his work, however small, added to their welfare. This dedication imparted a cosmic meaning to human life. As Simone Weil has said, a civilization based upon a sacred conception of vocation gives man a feeling of being deeply rooted in the universe.[2] Hegel conceived of history as an expression of a cosmic creative reason, and Josiah Royce sought to develop a similar viewpoint, regarding the history of the universe as the history of the development of a universal community.[3] Whitehead likewise conceived of the cosmos as a meaningful process consisting of the formation of increasingly complex societies.[4]

Tradition tends to gratify one of the greatest of all human desires—the wish to be remembered in one's absence, whether this be merely temporary departure or death. This explains to a large degree the desire of parents to have children. Indeed, in primitive societies, the creative instinct is mainly expressed in the desire to expand the family; this was the germ of the feeling that the meaning of life is to be part of history.[5] Similar conceptions were expressed by McDougall, who stressed that society consists of the dead to a larger extent than the living, in that, over countless generations, people of the past have struggled to create our present material and intellectual heritage.[6]

3. SYMBOLS OF HOME

In the most sublime sense, then, money was a symbol of eternal love, for the common meal was the focal point of the family tradition. Money at first represented the emotions and values associated with the home.

As a physical locale, the home is a spot where the surroundings and material objects constitute souvenirs or relics which evoke sentimental memories of warm relationships with the kinship group. Speaking more abstractly, the home is the mutual identification of each individual with a common tradition which gives each person the feeling of having roots.[7] Money was originally a religious symbol, and the first conceptions of religion are developed within an individual's home life. Religion, as Josiah Royce said, is "feeling at home in the universe." Greek religious ritual, we shall see, was originally an expression of the warm bonds among the members of the kinship group.[8]

The home centers around the figures of the parents, who are the carriers of the family tradition. The first heroes were the past members of the kinship group, whose memory was perpetuated in rite and myth. One of the factors which was responsible for the greatness of an ancient family was the vitality and moral virtue of its founder, and the character of the founder was perpetuated in later generations through the ancestral cult.

The carrying-over of the family tradition is accomplished by the child's identification with his parents. This identification, where the parents are genuinely creative individuals devoted to the promotion of the community, imbues the person with a deep source of inspiration that furnishes the basis for a fine moral character. Jung and his followers, particularly Baynes,[9] have emphasized the importance of tradition as an integrating force in an individual's psychic life.

One of the oldest folk symbols in the history of ancient Greece and Rome was the sacred hearth fire[10] at which the family meal was prepared. This holy fire had a strong emotional meaning for early men, for, as the focus of the mutual devotion of each individual to the welfare of the group in the division of labor, it symbolized the vitality of the community. Two of man's basic needs—warmth amidst numbing coldness, and a guide when lost—were provided by the flame, which gave comfort and security amongst the menacing forces of nature. Finally, as the point of distribution of the shared food, the hearth symbolized the rich, sentimental memories of the home life.[11]

4. PARENTAL IMAGES AND
MORAL DEVELOPMENT

The meaning of money was at first bound up with the mother and father images, for it is the parents who largely determine the character of the kinship group. Indeed, the early history of the monetary institution is to a great extent a study of the influence of parental images in primitive group psychology.

The first contact any individual has with the traditions of his community is in the child-mother relation, for the values of a culture are reflected in its infant-rearing practices. The relationship to a good mother establishes deep-rooted emotional-ideational attitudes toward the outer world and other people, and imbues a person with the ideal of a productive human relation. The mother image may for this reason come to be conceived as an expression of the creative forces of nature.

Psychoanalytic theory has largely been concerned with the pathology resulting from an adult's clinging to irrational aspects of the mother-child relation. However, it is obvious that the rational elements in this relation are of considerable importance in the development of an individual's moral values.

The mental, physical, and emotional vitality of an infant is a function of its having a stable love relationship,[12] and it is typically the mother who fulfills this need. From a psychological point of view, the first form of money is mother's milk. Studies of babies alone in hospitals reveal a clinical picture of retardation of growth, poor appetite, and other physical symptoms. Such children are listless, and smile and babble infrequently. Upon being returned to their parents, however, they immediately gain weight and exhibit more healthy reactions. The lack of maternal love, of which nursing is the main expression, causes both emotional and physical retardation. Dr. Margaret Ribble has illustrated these facts in her book, *The Rights of Infants*.[13]

The emotional relationship of infant to mother is of a co-operative nature, Ashley Montagu states, citing Alfred Adler's remark that "the first act of a new-born child—drinking from the mother's breast—is cooperation, and is as pleasant for the mother as for the child."[14] The child does not simply take from the mother, in the form of attention, warmth, and food, but it gives love to the mother, in the form of smiles and other types of affection. The very act of suckling is a giving on the part of the child, as well as a taking.

These infantile experiences of the sharing of food influence the child's later attitudes toward money, for the child who is deprived of adequate love tends to lack the capacity for entering into loving, i.e., moral relationships with others in later life. He tends to develop an unsocial, insecure, and hostile personality. The ability to give and receive affection is absent, and the individual is unable to understand and accept the necessity for imposing limitations on his own desires.[15] Modern psychiatry has shown that the pathological quest for money is often closely associated with the maternal image.[16]

The father likewise plays an important part in molding an individual's character. In his role as provider of food, he sets an example of dedicated sharing and loyal interdependence. It seems reasonable to suppose that many of a child's first conceptions of money and the division of labor are received from the efforts and renunciations made by his father and mother for his welfare. The joy in giving to others, and the capacity to appreciate gifts—these are the essences of money—are moral insights which the child first has the opportunity to learn from his parents.

The good parent causes the child to form a deep-rooted identification with the highest ideals of the culture. For this reason, in later life, the individual feels that a dishonorable action places him in disgrace; he experiences guilt, and feels cut off from the historical continuity of his group if he violates the ideals embodied in the tradition.

When parents embody the ideals of honor, justice, and love, an individual is enabled to develop character and moral insights. Despite the vices inherent in a hereditary aristocracy, it must be admitted that this type of ancestral tradition often leads to the emergence of extraordinarily high-minded individuals.[17] Certainly a family life which creates anxieties and real dangers for a growing child frequently causes him to practice deception and underhanded retaliation, stunting his capacity for sincerity and graciousness. Because the adult's attitudes toward money are often strongly influenced by his early relationships, it is desirable, from society's standpoint, for each individual to become capable of freeing himself from unhealthy childhood influences.[18]

5. PARENTAL IMAGES IN
ANCIENT GROUP PSYCHOLOGY

The ancient cities of Greece and Rome, we shall see, were artificial brotherhoods based on mutual identification with a common divine parent. Insofar as a society's deified parent-image embodies a creative tradition, we may speak of that society as a "holy community."

Apart from the superstition and immaturity manifested in in these city brotherhoods of antiquity, they consisted of a mutually dedicated fellowship, a loyal union of individuals who expressed their souls through their participation in the division of labor. Each fellow, modeling himself after an idealized parental figure embodying joyous cooperation, devoted his heart to the promotion of the group, thereby gratifying his deepest yearnings. The god or goddess worshiped by a brotherhood was, in its lofty aspect, the personification of the moral virtues that each person strived to emulate.

The heroes and gods that a community worships are very often personified as a father. George Washington is spoken of as "the father of his country." The Czar of Russia was the "little father," and the Germans regard their country as the "fatherland." The words "patriot" and "patriotism," which stem from the Latin *pater*, or "father," carry the connotation of devotion to the welfare of the community. The Roman god "Jupiter" stems from the Greek "Zeus pater."

In a similar manner, the goddesses of ancient times were venerated as maternal divinities. The *alma mater* songs of modern universities, in which the college is personified as a cherishing maternal figure, illustrate the emotional fervor of the communicants in the ancient religious fellowships toward their common ideal of creativity. The Columbia University anthem, beginning with the phrase, "Mother, stayed on rock eternal," might well have been a hymn to Athena sung at a solemn religious ritual on the Acropolis.

6. THE HIGHER SIGNIFICANCE OF PHALLIC SYMBOLS

Ancient money, originating with the family meal, expressed the feelings of kinship, love, and creativity symbolized by early man's gods and goddesses; and these emotions and ideas, with the evolution of money, were carried over, as we shall see, into the symbolism of the first coins.

The holy hearth fire representing the sharing of food among the family circle was a phallic symbol to the men of antiquity, and this sexual symbolism was sometimes carried over into the early forms of coined money. To understand this imagery we must grasp the significance of the generative organs to the people of early times.

In antiquity the main expression of man's creative drive was his dedication to the continuation of his family, or its extension, the clan. The entire life of the individual was subordinated to the perpetuation of the kinship group; in this way, every person achieved an immortality through his descendants. In early Greece and Rome, celibacy was a crime, and a wife could be divorced if she were sterile.[19] The Bible contains many illustrations of the importance which men attached to the expansion of their family group.

The sexual symbolism found so often in ancient religions, in which the male or female genitals were venerated, was hence not merely the expression of sensual desire, but was an embodiment of the creative forces in man by which the kinship community was perpetuated. Sexual symbols embodied the tradition or immortality of the family. The amulets representing the phallus or the vagina, found in the cultures of antiquity, were magical means for obtaining immortality. As the means for perpetuating the family, the sexual organs symbolized the lineage.[20] The ancestral god for this reason was often represented in phallic form.

The snake, as a phallic symbol, frequently was regarded as a spirit of generation, even of immortality, in ancient times, and therefore was believed to be sacred, filled with *mana*.[21] In Rome, the *genius*, or ancestral soul, was a serpent.[22] Likewise, the Greek *heroes* (ancestral souls) took the form of snakes, as did the souls of the early Athenian kings.[23]

Many of the gods of classical antiquity originated as phallic representations. Indeed, the tree and pillar cult, which played an important role in early Greek culture, was phallic in nature; the first representations of the gods were simply these rude tree trunks or stones, which later, with the advent of civilization, became statues and idols. The sacred fire also appeared in some instances as a phallic symbol.[24]

The cowry shells which have served as money in primitive cultures in many parts of the world were valued basically because of their magical powers in conferring fertility upon women.[25] This potency resulted from the similarity of the shape of the shells to the external aspect of the female genitals. The cowry shell was employed as money in early Egypt, which some writers have regarded as the birthplace of this world-wide practice. According to G. Elliot Smith, this amulet represented the Great Mother, the creator of the human family.[26] Thus, one of the earliest forms of money had both a rational and an irrational symbolism; rational in that it represented man's desire to commit his energies to the tradition of the perpetuation of human life, and irrational in that it represented magical ideas connected with the mother.

four

MYTHIC HEROES
AND GODS

1. IMAGES OF THE HERO

Throughout the history of money, the images on each country's coins have often consisted of depictions of that nation's traditional heroes. Today, for example, our penny bears a picture of Lincoln, our nickel Jefferson, and our dime a picture of Franklin D. Roosevelt.

Every culture has its mythic heroes embodying its great traditions—godlike figures of the past whose might and courage triumphed over overwhelming odds to perpetuate the ideals of the society. Even the American "western" movies have as an almost invariant theme a lone rider whose sagacity, courage, and fast shooting ultimately brings the rustlers and murderers to a fair trial for their crimes. These heroic myths of "lawless frontier days" are a healthy sign of the persistence of the English tradition which holds that no man can be deprived of life, liberty, or property without due process of law.

But mythology has adolescent, even infantile aspects, along with its mature, admirable qualities. All great men have human frailties, and to revere excessively even the finest individual is generally the result of a child-like over-evaluation of the power and moral character of the father. Much mythology is of this nature.

The images on money may symbolize either the ideals represented by a heroic figure, or may serve to honor an individual who in reality is corrupt or cowardly. Ancient money, as we shall see, had a diversity of meanings, for any human relation is a composite of motivations, a mixture of ideas and emotions stemming from many sources, both conscious and unconscious.

2. HERO, MYTH, AND TRADITION

The hero is an individual whose moral virtues, intelligence, and strength enable him to face and overcome a crisis which threatens the community. In a lofty sense, he can be said to express the creative powers of nature, for these vital forces are personified in his actions at a time of peril. By expressing his soul, the hero lives the fullest possible life; he is the truly religious person.

The character of the hero brings out in other individuals an awareness of their deeper potentialities for emotional experience. He creates in others a feeling of exaltation, a desire to consecrate their lives to a cause which dominates lesser interests. This type of inspiration is infantile only when it causes a loss of rationality and a regression to immature ideas. A genuinely great person evokes mature enthusiasm, and stirs men's souls to higher achievements. The hero embodies the tradition of the community. Saga and legend over the centuries extend his exploits, magnify his powers, and ultimately transform him into a god.

Participation in the common meal, it will become increasingly apparent, symbolized early man's identification with the mythic hero, apotheosized into a deity. And as the family repast evolved into the first forms of coinage, the pictorial images of these hero-gods became the types stamped upon the coins. Money, like the Holy Grail, began as a sacred distribution of food, which in later centuries was symbolically represented by a religious relic or souvenir serving as a medal of honor.

The tradition of devotion to the advancement of civilization symbolized by money was first sensed by ancient man in the genealogy of his family: the first heroes were the revered ancestors who founded and helped to perpetuate the kinship group. The deeds of these honored dead, recounted from generation to generation, furnished myths, models for moral identification, which inspired the descendants of these gods with the strength of devotion necessary for the perpetuation and progress of the lineage.

It is true that an immature, narrow nationalism may arise from the mass acceptance of a myth expressing false moral values. The philosopher Ernst Cassirer[1] has discussed these regressive myths and the corrupt political ideals produced by the intoxication of the masses. However, a rational myth or tradition correctly and without exaggeration recounts the life of a truly extraordinary person of emotional depth, courage, and virtue. By inspiring the members of the community to identify with this hero, such a myth imparts vitality to a culture, for it promotes a character structure which carries on the ideas of the civilization.

The mythic hero, or god, symbolizes the creative continuity of the culture. Insofar as he stimulates others to emulate him, thereby perpetuating the ancient virtues, the hero is immortal.[2] Tradition enables people to derive inspiration from the contemplation of the past,[3] and provides an ideal of moral conduct for each member of the group to imitate. It is correct to point out, as did Bergson,[4] that much of popular morality and religion is derived from uncritical acceptance of custom. However, the free, mature individual accepts these ideas on the basis of personal reflection and experience, and in this respect a myth serves as a guide to broader religious insight.

A healthy tradition inspires an individual to find the courage to fight for the things he loves, and provides a standard of honor which springs from the real needs of a creative society. It possesses a sweeping power, imparting vitality and majesty to a culture. A mature myth, Malinowski[5] said, gives the culture rational direction and unity of purpose toward genuinely higher goals.

Religious rituals and temples serve as public ceremonies and monuments which remind every individual of the tradition of progress to which he belongs. In identifying himself with a rational myth, an individual lives with the feeling that his life is meaningful and has direction. From this moral vigor a culture draws its vitality. The role of tradition in perpetuating ideals is well exemplified in military groups, despite their authoritarian nature. An American officer, Lovette, writes of Annapolis:

> The value of tradition as built by the Navy Spirit is inestimable. The air of Annapolis breathes with traditions from the time one takes his oath in Memorial Hall to the hour he leaves the Naval Academy. "Don't give up the ship," "We have met the enemy and they are ours" . . . these and countless other reminders of the highest in character are constant models toward which the impressionable young man shapes his ideals. The Herndon Monument, the names, the stories of our great service are the solid foundations upon which is built the character and loyalty that characterizes our esprit de corps.[6]

Myth has its roots in religion, and the purpose of religious ritual is to renew the vigor of the culture by inspiring each individual to revivify his identification with the tradition. Through ceremonies which commemorate the lives of the heroes, the commitment of each successive generation to the progress of the community is heightened. As Durkheim* said:

> The mythology of a group is the system of beliefs common to this group. The traditions whose memory it perpetuates express the way in which society represents man and the world; it is a moral system and a cosmology as well as a history. So the rite serves and can serve only to sustain the vitality of these beliefs, to keep them from being effaced from memory and, in sum, to revivify the most essential elements of the collective consciousness. Through it, the group periodically renews the sentiment which it has of itself and of its unity; at the same time, individuals are strengthened in their social natures. The glorious souvenirs which are made to live again before their eyes, and with which they feel that they have a kinship, give them a feeling of strength and of confidence: a man is surer of his faith when he sees to how distant a past it goes back and what great things it has inspired.[7]

3. MEDALS, MONUMENTS, AND MYTHS

The essence of primitive religion behind superstitious practices and beliefs is the identification of the members of a group with the creative forces in nature. The history of the great men whose outstanding religious commitment has maintained and enriched the community is commemorated by the rituals at the temples.

Indeed, the rational function of all sacred objects and holy places is to keep alive in the memory of the community the inspiring identification with the culture's heroes. Ancestor worship, in its rational aspect, is an essential part of tradition insofar as it consists of a recognition and admiration of the moral virtues of past members of the community. The religion of the dead so frequently encountered in primitive cultures has as its

---

* For Durkheim, religion is mainly the outwardly projected image of the group unity, whereas this book regards religion as an objectively existing cosmic force, from which the culture draws its vitality.

function the revitalization of each person's feeling that his primary duties in life are to his lineage.[8]

The first coins were actually medals, and only in the course of later developments did they become media of exchange which circulated among traders in the marketplace. And medals are essentially religious symbols, in that they represent service and loyalty to the community. They commemorate past heroism, and inspire the living generation to perpetuate the sacred tradition.

Medals play a role similar to monuments—they memorialize the deeds which have helped to preserve great ideals, and inspire others to model their lives after the heroes. In his dedication to the book *The Medal of Honor of the United States Army,* a President of the United States declares:

> . . . to perpetuate in memory the deeds of courage and selflessness for which the Medal has been awarded and to give the American people a fuller understanding of the ideal for which the Medal of Honor stands in the history of our Army and of our country.
>
> It is to the men—living and dead—who have won this high honor during the history of our nation that this book is dedicated.
>
> May the courage and heroism of which this Medal is a symbol always remind us of our debt to these men, and clearly point to the personal responsibility which every American has today to share in the work of helping to build a healthy and peaceful world. . . .[9]

The beginnings of coinage were in the temples, and the distribution of these sacred medals evolved from the distribution of the food by the priests who presided over the common meal.

The religious leader in primitive culture, insofar as he performs a rational function, is an individual who feels within himself the creative forces of nature, and who identifies himself with the tradition symbolized by the heroic ancestors. As contrasted with the frequently corrupt tribal magician, he is a person of outstanding moral character, wisdom, and courage.

In ancient Greece and Rome, one of the principal duties of the priest was to preside at the holy repasts. The common meal was for many centuries indistinguishable from the ancestor worship; and, in officiating at these rituals, the priest helped to renew the community, strengthen the moral ties among individuals, and give a deeper meaning to living. The priest stirred men's souls, inspiring within each individual the exalted sense of being a loyal participant in the group's traditions. He kept alive in the hearts of the communicants the richness of life achieved by the respected dead, and invoked the image of a great man with whom to identify. The priest perpetuated the myth of the hero.

five

THE CITY
BROTHERHOOD

1. SPIRITS OF THE DEAD

In the first chapter, we declared that money represents the Christmas spirit. The fact is that Christmas literally signifies a mass, or sacred meal, held to commemorate the deity who died heroically for the sake of the community; and the Christmas spirit is an identification with the ideal of universal love contained in the Christian tradition.

Most of us are familiar with the masses held to honor the saints, but few people are aware that such commemorative ritual meals existed for millennia before the Christian era, and formed an integral part of the numerous religions from which Christi-

» 47

anity emerged at the time of the disintegration of the Roman Empire. The sacred repast, or love feast, commemorating the souls of the departed heroes was the basic institution of ancient society, serving as the core of the religious and political life of the time, much as similar sacraments in later centuries were to become the central rite in the religion of Christianity. Thus, at the time of its origin in the sacred meal, money was an expression of man's quest for the universal fellowship of mankind.

When we use the term Christmas "spirit," we certainly do not have in mind some ghostly apparition; we simply mean an idea or feeling. But early man, ignorant and superstitious as he was, had entirely different conceptions of the nature of the world, and actually believed in the existence of disembodied souls and the spirits of the dead. Today, the custom of Halloween (All Hallows Evening) is an occasion for children; but just two or three centuries ago ghosts and haunted houses were realities to adults, and doubtless there even now persist backward peasant areas in the midst of our scientific civilization where such beliefs linger. It was not so long ago that people were hanged for witchcraft in Massachusetts. The truth is that the existence of a cult of the dead is a regularly found, perhaps universal phenomenon among primitive people, and many anthropologists have studied the survivals of these ideas and practices in the folkways of higher cultures.

Now there is obviously much that is quite reasonable in these old superstitions. For example, the phrase, "The Spirit of '76," instantly conjures up in our minds the famous picture of three ragged but indomitable heroes of the American Revolution. We do not, of course, in any sense believe that the souls of these soldiers are hovering around us in a supernatural miasma, but we do carry around, within our minds, an image of these heroic figures of American history. Ancient man, however, failed to distinguish clearly between ideas within his mind and that which existed in objective reality; he projected his memories into the environment, and these remembered images, conceived to be outside of himself, gave rise to the spirits and ghosts which were believed to populate the external world.

Apart from the magical aspects of the cult of the dead, these beliefs were quite sensible. For we are continually surrounded, in our conscious life, by innumerable memories of people we have known in the past, and whose influence still persists in our daily decisions and plans. Psychoanalysis calls these memories the "superego," and demonstrates the tremendous power which these past human relations exert upon our present ideas, emotions, and behavior. Much of the superego is unconscious, repressed from awareness, for it consists of guilty rememberances of feared or hated people, some of whom were perhaps kinfolk. Projected into the environment by primitive man, these repressed memories became evil demons and souls of the dead returning to haunt the survivors. In short, they were, to a large extent, the conscience of ancient man.

The noted French legal historian Fustel de Coulanges[1] has shown in his famous book *The Ancient City* that this externally projected conscience was a major determinant of the life and social institutions of the people of Greek and Roman antiquity. The ancestral spirits, representing the tradition of the community, were important historical forces, often exerting a decisive influence upon the course of human affairs. The family meal, presided over by the father, symbolized this tradition, and was the origin of the common meal of the city, officiated over by a priestly king. As we shall see, it was here, in this public sacred communion, that coinage originated.

2. FOOD RITUALS FOR DEAD HEROES

The ancient Greeks and Romans believed that, upon burying a body, the soul was likewise being interred, and would continue to live under ground, experiencing pleasures and pains like a living thing. For this reason, various objects which the soul would need, such as clothing, utensils, and food, were often buried with the dead man. Horses and slaves were sometimes slaughtered and entombed with him, in the belief that they would continue to serve him after death.

An unburied soul, however, had no resting place, and became a wandering spirit. Such a soul became a phantom, seeking in vain the offerings and food which it required. It became an evil spirit, tormenting the living, bringing diseases, ruining harvests, and appearing in ghastly apparitions to warn the survivors to give its body a tomb.

But mere burial was not sufficient, for a soul entombed without the proper rites and formulae was also lost forever. Just as certain rites could be used for the purpose of temporarily raising the dead from the sepulcher, so there were rites to keep the soul permanently in its tomb. The souls living under ground required meals on certain days of the year. At such times, the tomb was surrounded with large wreaths, as well as with cakes, fruits, flowers, milk, or wine. Sometimes the blood of a victim was added. In front of every tomb were altars designed for the immolation of the victim and the cooking of its flesh. These beliefs and rituals, Fustel de Coulanges wrote, ". . . exercised empire over man during a great number of generations. They governed men's minds . . . they governed societies even, and . . . the greater part of the domestic and social institutions of the ancients was derived from this source."[2]

3. THE FAMILY RELIGION

In the home of every Greek and Roman there was an altar, or hearth, upon which was kept burning a sacred fire. It was a solemn obligation for the head of the family to keep this fire from being extinguished. The fire was a divinity to which the ancients made offerings as to a god—gifts such as flowers, fruits, incense, wine, and sacrificial victims. The meals of the family were sacred rites, in which each person entered into communion with the deity. Having prepared their nourishment, the participants offered prayers, which were repeated at the end of the repast. The god was believed to preside at the meal; and, by casting food and wine into the fire, the ancient man gave the god his portion.

The worship of the dead was one with the religion of the holy fire at the sacred hearth; it was a son's duty to make the libations and sacrifices to the soul of his father and all of his ancestors. These funeral offerings established a powerful and inseparable bond between the son and his predecessors. The dead were regarded as gods, and the tombs of the ancestors were hence the temples of these divinities. The human souls deified after death, and living in the tomb near the family house, were called *daimons* or *heroes* by the Greeks and *lares, manes* or *genii* by the Latins. In this way, the ancestral gods remained in the midst of their descendants, and, if properly honored by worship, continued to act as they had in earthly life, protecting, giving advice, and consoling.

The ancient family was a religious association, and a person was a member of a family by virtue of the fact that he shared in the religion of the sacred fire. The ancient Greek word for "family" is very significant; it means "that which is near a hearth."

It was necessary for a family to perpetuate itself forever, for if the kinship group died out there would be no one to offer the funeral repasts at the tomb, and the entire series of dead ancestors would become unhappy, wandering spirits. A man was not born for himself, but for the sake of his family; a person's main reason for existence was his obligation to continue the worship. The hearth, or altar, once established upon the ground, was believed to be there for eternity. Land did not belong to the individual in ancient times—it belonged to the ancestral tradition. The head of a family held the land in trust for the entire lineage, those dead, living, and those yet to be born. The field was part of the body of the family, and to attempt to detach a family from its land was to offend its gods.

Appreciation and identification with the devotion of past generations to the welfare of the community were the rational aspects of the cult of the dead. For a culture, both materially and nonmaterially, is a monument to the efforts, renunciations, and pains of the past members of the group. The souls of the dead were simply the enduring memories of these individuals in the minds of the living, and the rituals at the sacred hearth functioned to inspire later generations with the same greatness of soul as was possessed by the heroic ancestors. The rootedness of such sentiments in the hearts of men is illustrated centuries later in the Gettysburg Address, which was a type of votive offering in a funeral rite.

"It is rather for us to be here dedicated to the great task remaining before us; that from these honored dead we take increased devotion to that cause to which they gave the last full measure of devotion."

Lincoln's speech illustrates the major function of myth: to inspire the living to identify themselves with the souls of the dead, in the resolve to perpetuate the tradition which constitutes the driving force behind the culture.

4. FAMILY AUTHORITY AND RELIGION

The laws of the family were not derived from those of the city, for the city did not yet exist. Ancient law originated in the ancestor worship of the family, stemming from religious beliefs which prevailed throughout primitive Graeco-Roman culture.

The supreme authority in the household, controlling the actions even of the father, was the domestic religion. The father was the first priest, leading the rituals, slaying the victim, and pronouncing the prayers. The lineage and its worship were perpetuated through him; he represented the entire series of ancestors—he personified the tradition. When death occurred, he too became a god to be worshiped by his descendants. Thus, each person's life was strictly governed by the ancestral tradition handed down from his father.

The sons, under the domestic religion of early times, remained subjected to the father during their entire life. Even as a married man and the father of children, the son was under parental authority. The ancestor worship established the family as a little society with its own chief and government.

The most important laws administered by the father were homely in nature, consisting to a large extent of regulations for the distribution of food at the sacred meal. The first type of pay was the shared food, and the manner of distributing this edible money was the first form taken by the science of management.

The first industrial unit, the *oikos,* or house, was a religious economic system; and, as Seebohm[3] says, the supreme duty of each individual was to commit himself completely, sacrificing all personal motivations, to the perpetuation of his family unit. In the household economy, we find the beginnings of taxation, the tithe, in the contribution of each person to the common meal. The word "liturgy" meant in the earliest times the gift made to the household economy; and the first taxes were gifts of food for this religious communion.

The sacred meal was an early form of the division of labor, or mutual aid, in which each individual underwent strenuous efforts, renunciations, and pains for the good of the community. It symbolized the result of these sacrifices, the deep gratification of feeling at one with a community of persons who respected each other and shared memories of common toil and danger.

The meaning of sacrifice was thus identical with devoted work. The common meal expressed man's joy in cooperating with others; and the mutual love and gratitude manifested in the division of labor constituted a communion. The sharing of the flesh of the sacrificial animal with the ancestral souls had a commemorative function, for this ritual was basically the expression of gratitude to the past generations whose efforts had made the present community possible. It is true that in some instances the living did not partake of the common food with the dead, merely offering the nourishment to the deceased soul; but the feeling of emotional unity nevertheless existed. In the sacred repast shared by the god and his worshipers, all of the past, present, and future members of the culture entered into communion with one another and with the creative forces expressed in the family tradition.

5. THANKS GIVING

Now the food communion rituals were in a sense gift exchanges, or loving commerce, carried on between the community and its deified ancestors, in the form of sacrificial gifts, called "dedications," or "votive offerings." These gifts were essentially requests for the god's blessing. The deity was invoked, and asked for a favor, such as a good harvest, or success in some hazardous undertaking. If the request was granted, the divinity was thanked by a suitable sacrificial repast.

We are familiar with a similar practice in modern America, namely the Thanksgiving dinner. This feast day was not a custom that sprang up directly from the minds of the early settlers, but like many of their beliefs was an old folk tradition brought over from Europe by the colonists. In fact, throughout the world, in primitive and advanced cultures alike, harvest festivals are a frequently encountered custom in which people celebrate the good crops with a common meal. The feast appears to be one of man's universal ways of commemorating such occasions, which we have come to call "festive." In its lofty sense, the thanksgiving ritual is an expression of the individual's desire to reaffirm the creative powers within himself; in ancient times, these feelings of inner strength and vitality were outwardly projected, and were personified by the ancestral heroes to whom the offerings, or dedications, were made. Participation in the ritual also intensified the mutual bonds of loyalty among the members of the group, thereby revitalizing the spirit of creative cooperation which gave the community its vigor.

At times the votive offering was a begging for forgiveness for a transgression of the ancestral laws, in which the members of the communion, called "votaries," sought atonement (literally "at one-ment"). These purificatory sacrifices had both an expiatory and a propitiatory significance. In the former, the communicants sought to atone for the offense they had committed against the god, i.e., against the welfare of the community; in the latter the community sought to avert the wrath of the god by offering a gift or by punishing an offending individual. In Greece the practice existed of loading the sins of the community upon an individual called the *pharmakos,* who was sacrificed as a scapegoat. The frequent offering of humans as expiatory sacrifices in ancient times resulted partially from the fact that criminal law was originally part of the ancestral cult, an aspect of the community's relationship to its god.

The basic meaning of the purificatory sacrifice was to express man's sense of guilt for his inability to live up to the moral ideals embodied in the tradition. As Erich Fromm has said, guilt is our inner reaction when we fail to act in a manner suitable to the realization of our deepest potentialities.[4] When the ancient individual behaved contrary to the promotion of the community, he tended to lose direction. He felt that he was no longer part of the sacred tradition, and began to feel that life was meaningless and futile. By making a dedication, a person sought to regain his sense of communion with the ancestral souls.

6. THE FORMATION OF
LARGER COMMUNITIES

The invoking of the deity by a votive offering had as its basic rationale the revivification of the sense of unity between the individual and his creative needs. This rite was the origin of the prayers and invocations with which we still begin the most solemn of our public ceremonies. The ancient Greeks and Romans began most legal proceedings with an animal sacrifice, in order to invoke the blessing of the gods. The purpose of this ritual was to evoke in the minds of the participants the creative feelings which would lend honor and mutual respect to the civic procedure. Ancient men carried over into the larger communities the same piety, creative dedication, as at first existed in the family.

The earliest community other than the family which we encounter in antiquity is a kinship group called the *gens*, or clan. All members of the gens had the same worship, performed sacrifices at a common altar, and participated in the same rituals at a common tomb of a deified ancestor. It was each person's duty to perpetuate the worship of the gens from generation to generation, and every man was required to leave sons behind him to do likewise. Each gens had a chief, who at the same time was its judge, priest, and military commander.

According to Fustel de Coulanges, the primitive gens was merely an enlargement of the family, comprising either a single branch or several stems. The family was the original form of social organization, existing with its ancestor worship, sacred fire, and laws, long before any larger social bodies came into being. The gens developed by the expansion of the family, several subsidiary branches remaining grouped around the main branch near the sacred fire and the common tomb.

Despite the fact that the domestic religion forbade two families from mingling or uniting with each other, it was possible for several families, each without sacrificing its special ancestor worship and rituals, to join for the celebration of another worship common to all. Several families would unite to form a group called by the Greeks, a *phratria*, and by the Romans a *curia*. There was no tie of birth among the constituent families; but, with the formation of these larger social units, there resulted a growth of religious ideas and the idea of a divinity superior to that of the household, one who was common to all, and who watched over the entire group.

The confederated families raised an altar to this deity, lit a sacred fire, and founded a worship. Every cury or phratry had an altar and a protecting divinity. The religious procedures here were the same as those in the family: there was a common meal, whose nourishment was prepared upon the altar; there were prayers recited during the repast; and the deity, who was believed to be present, received his share of the food and drink. The chief of a phratry or cury was called a phratriarch or curion, whose main duty was to preside at the sacrificial rituals. The phratry had regular assemblies and a tribunal. It had its god, its worship, priest, legal body, and government; in every respect, it was a body modeled upon the family organization.

Now it would sometimes happen that several phratries, or curies, would unite to form a tribe. This new association also had its religion, its altar, and protecting divinity. The god of the tribe was usually the same in nature as that of the family and phratry; it was a deified man, called a *hero,* from whom the tribe took its name. Called an "eponymous hero" by the Greeks, this god had his annual festal day when the entire tribe participated in a common meal. Like the gens and the phratry, the tribe held assemblies which made laws binding its members. Ruled by a king, the tribe was an independent body subject to no other social power.

7. THE ORIGIN OF THE CITY

Just as several phratries might unite to form a tribe, so several tribes might confederate. The alliance of tribes constituted the first city, and it was here that, in embryonic form, our modern economic institutions began to take shape.

There was no single reason why a group of tribes would unite to form a city, nor did this enlargement of social units occur in an orderly, logical fashion. Sometimes a confederation was voluntary, sometimes imposed by the superior force of one tribe, and sometimes the union of tribes was the result of the powerful will of one man. But the bond of the new association was always religion. The confederated tribes never failed to light a sacred fire and perform common rituals.

Practices which continued for many centuries attest to the

manner in which the ancient cities arose. For example, the army of the primitive city was divided into tribes, curies, and families, so that, in the words of one ancient writer, ". . . the warrior has for a neighbor in the combat one with whom, in time of peace, he has offered the libation and sacrifice at the same altar." In the early days of Rome, we find the populace voting by curies and by gens. The religious worship of Rome was presided over by six vestals, one for each tribe. At Athens, the archon offered the sacrifice in the name of the whole city, but in the rituals he had as many assistants as there were tribes.

The gods of the city were in some instances the divinities of the leading family. The Demeter of Eleusis remained the god of the family of the Eumolpidae, and the Athena of the Acropolis at Athens belonged to the Butadae family. When the household divinities became city gods, the family retained the priesthood as a hereditary privilege.

The ancient city must not be construed as an agglomeration of men living mingled together within the same enclosure. In the earliest days, the city was not a place of habitation; rather, it was the sanctuary where the gods lived—it was a fortress, the center of the confederation, the residence of the king and priests, and the place where justice was administered. But people did not live there. For many years, they lived outside of the city in isolated communities, each occupying their own land, and holding their domestic worship under the direction of the father.

The first assembly of the ancient city was composed of the heads of families—the *paters*. These men, united, constituted the city, but each remained master in his gens, his little kingdom. Only on certain days did the paters gather in the city to deliberate upon policies, or to take part in a religious sacrifice.

The city was formed when all of the constituent families, phratries, and tribes for one reason or another became united under the same tradition .The founding of the city was a religious act, and the city was the sanctuary for the common worship. Each individual retained the feeling of being rooted in the land of his ancestors. In establishing the site for Rome, Romulus is said to have dug a small circular trench into which he and his companions each threw a clod of earth from his native country. This trench was called *mundus,* meaning "the region of the *manes*"—the place where the souls of the ancestors dwelled. By throwing in the clod of earth, each man believed that he was enclosing the souls of his ancestors. Since these souls required a perpetual worship with funeral sacrifices, Romulus set up an altar on this spot, and lighted a fire upon it. This became the holy fire of Rome, around which the city arose.

The founder of a city was the person who had brought the gods to the city, established the sacred hearth, and had caused the sacred fire to burn. Every city of ancient Greece and Italy had a temple at which the founder was worshiped, and where sacrifices to him were offered. He eventually was regarded as a common ancestor of the inhabitants of the city; and, as a deified hero, was the center of the religious cult.

Just as the domestic altar established a close sentimental tie among the members of a family, so the tutelary deity of the city, who was worshiped at the common municipal altar, provided the basis for social cohesion among the members of the con-federated tribes. The city altar was enclosed within a building called a "prytaneum" by the Greeks, and the "Temple of Vesta" by the Romans. The home of the sacred fire was the most sacred place in the city.

Each city had its own hierarchy of priests, its own sacred liturgies and rituals. The gods of the city were regarded as protectors; men sought their assistance when in danger, and offered thanks for prosperity. Just as each family had its domestic religion, each city had its national religion. A city, like a little church, had its gods, its dogmas, and its worship. These crude beliefs in ancestral protecting divinities were held by the most intelligent people of ancient times, and exercised a vast influence upon the laws, institutions, and history of early Greece and Rome.

8. THE SACRED MEALS OF THE CITY

City life, cold, alien, and heartless as it has often become, began with the transference of kinship feelings to all members of the enlarged social unit. Men retained their identification with the creative forces of nature, as expressed in the holy tradition of the city. The ideal of loving, giving and taking was extended, if only in a germinal aspect, to include all who worshiped at the prytaneum.

For the most important ritual of the city religion was a public meal at which all of the members of the community participated in a repast honoring the protective divinity. These common meals were a universal feature of the city worship throughout Greece, and it was believed that the safety of the city was contingent upon the performance of this sacrificial communion ritual. The eating of food prepared upon an altar was the first form which man gave to the religious act. Human association was a religion; its symbol was the common meal.

A description of these sacred repasts is contained in the *Odyssey*. At nine tables, each seating 500 citizens of Pylos, the meal, called the feast of the gods, was held, beginning and ending with libations and prayers. Each group immolated nine bulls in honor of the deities. This custom is mentioned in the oldest of Athenian traditions.

In addition to these huge municipal banquets at which the entire population assembled during solemn festivals, the religion also prescribed the holding of sacred meals every day. These were held within the prytaneum, in the presence of the sacred fire and the protecting gods, by men chosen to eat together as representatives of the entire population. It was believed that the omission of this communion ritual, even for a single day, might cause the city to lose the favor of the gods. The common meal began with a prayer and a libation, and hymns were sung during the repast.

9. KINGSHIP AND ANCIENT LAW

The political institutions of the ancient city were not based upon the deliberations of an assembly, but were part of every man's religious belief.

The priest of the city hearth was called "king," "prytane," or "archon." The term "prytane" was derived from the fact that he was the priest of the prytaneum, or local hearth. This king was, above all, the chief of the worship: he kept up the fire, offered the sacrifices, uttered the prayers, and presided at the common meals. Just as the family authority fell on the father, as the priest of the domestic hearth, so in the city the high priest of the prytaneum was simultaneously the politcal chief.

Since primitive man believed that his fortune was a function of the good will of the deities, he found himself dependent upon the priest, who acted as moderator between the gods and himself. The priest alone, through his knowledge of the rituals, could influence the divinity, and was hence of great power in the affairs of men. By virtue of his ability to call upon the gods for protection, the priest was acknowledged as magistrate, judge, and military chief.

The laws of the city priest-kingship stemmed from the rules of the religious rituals. The founder, who had established the sacred fire, was the first priest; and, in early days, heredity provided the rule for succession to the priesthood. The magistrate of the ancient city was also a priest, and he therefore had the title of king, prytane, or archon. The Athenian archons began their duty at the Acropolis by offering a sacrifice to the city deity, and were required to wear a crown of leaves upon their head. Indeed, the expression used by the Greeks to designate the magistrates was "those who are to accomplish the sacrifice."

Primitive law was part of religion, the ancient legal codes being a collection of rites, liturgies, and prayers, mixed with legislative regulations. The laws concerning property and succession were intermingled with directions for sacrifices, burials, and ancestor worship.

The code of the Twelve Tables, for example, contained exact and scrupulous rules concerning the interment of the dead. Solon's laws gave directions for the order of animal sacrifices, the price of victims, and the manner in which the deceased were to be worshiped. Since nearly every action a person made in his lifetime was controlled to some extent by religion, only the person versed in the ancestor worship could know the law. For this reason, the first lawyers were the priests: law and religion were one.

10. POLITICAL INJUSTICE
IN THE ANCIENT CITY

The ancient city was not a democracy; it was ruled by the heads of the great families. Insofar, however, as these powerful gens perpetuated the traditional moral virtues, which tended to be forgotten with the rise of the commercial classes, the aristocracy performed a vital social function later taken over by the universal religions of imperial Rome.[5] In fact, the word "aristocracy" meant in ancient Greece "the rule of the best people." For four centuries, from the death of Cedrus to the time of Solon, all authority in Athens was wielded by the clans of the Eupatridae. The term "Eupatrid" meant "well-fathered."

As a matter of fact, the word "gentleman" itself originally signified a member of a gens. The aristocratic ideal of the man of integrity, free from vanity and the desire for petty gain, and independent of the need to conform, appears in all lasting societies, however much in reality the heads of the great families may be arrogant, selfish, or decadent. Participation in the sacred food communion symbolizing the religious beliefs of the aristocracy signified not merely a "false class identification" with the exploitative rulers, but, to some extent, an identification with genuine moral ideals.

It must be granted, however, that in actuality a major part of the population consisted of slaves, and the lower classes were unjustly suppressed, often forcibly. To some degree, the Marxist doctrine held true in those times, in that the ancient religion, which was largely a continuation of the family ancestral cults, was an instrument for maintaining the power of the ruling kinship groups. As for the common meal, very likely many of the participants by no means felt a sense of loving communion in being present, but instead hated the patriarchal authority to which they were forced to submit for the sake of the miserable portions of food doled out to keep them from starvation.

For many centuries, the people were constrained from attacking the aristocrats because of their respect and fear of the religion of the city fathers—habits of mind from which they could not free themselves. But as commercial eminence, through the centuries, increasingly became the principle of power and status, the nobility became merely a hallowed memory, and the decaying aristocracy helplessly mourned the passing of the old values, and the godlessness of man. The great families continued reverently to perpetuate the domestic religion and the worship of their sacred ancestors, but no attempt was made to restore the ancient religion to its full strength. Eventually, the reforms of Cleisthenes at Athens, and Servius at Rome, established a democratic power structure, based on locality rather than on kinship.

As time went on, the old religion of the dead fell more and more into oblivion, and by the fifth century B.C. reflective individuals had completely abandoned the old beliefs. The masses of the people would continue for centuries to worship the dead, but among an increasing number of people, the rituals were becoming meaningless practices. The public hearth of the city, the prytaneum, lost emotional significance; men forgot that the sacred fire symbolized the spirits of the national ancestors, founders, and heroes. The holy flame was kept up, the public meals were held, and the old hymns were sung—for people still did not dare to free themselves completely from the old religion—but hardly anyone understood what these rituals signified. As the centuries passed, the ancient traditions were gradually synthesized into the new cults of the Roman Empire, and ultimately emerged, revivified, in a higher form, in the religion of Christianity.

PART 3

Kinship Feelings in
Fertility Rituals

six

PARENT IMAGES AND FERTILITY SPIRITS

1. SYMBOLS ON COINS

The images, or types, on coins are no mere decorations invented by the idle imagination of an artist, but are ideas of great emotional significance, often with a history extending back for thousands of years. Such heraldic decorations found on coins as the winged disk, laurel wreath, fleur-de-lis, or eagle can be traced to the earliest times and, like the cross, originated as symbols of traditions that still persist, sometimes becoming vital forces in modern mass psychology.

Many of the early coins bore types that displayed either the head of a god or some well-recognized symbol, called an "attribute," that magically represented a deity. On the coins of ancient Croton, for instance, the symbol of Apollo was the tripod, an object that was the special property of this divinity, under whose protection the city had been founded. Artemis was represented by the bee on the coins of Ephesus. On the coins of the city of Aegina, we find the tortoise of Astarte, at Cnidus the lion of Cybele, and at Rhaucus in Crete the trident of Poseidon.

These attributes can in most instances be traced back to the association of the deity with notions of food, fertility, and prosperity. This tendency survives in many of our modern coins, as for example the penny of the United States, with a spray of vegetation on one side, and on the reverse an image of that hero and father figure of American tradition, Abraham Lincoln. In a similar manner, an old Athenian coin, the tetradrachm, had as its type an image of Athena, the patroness of that ancient city; on the reverse was shown an olive spray with a crescent moon. Athena in primitive times was a moon goddess identified with the olive tree, and underlying this symbolism were early cosmological ideas stemming from the belief that parental deities were connected with the growth of the crops.

Securing an adequate supply of food was a continual problem for primitive man, and to a large extent his emotional life and world view resulted from his association of nourishment with the mother and father figures. Indeed, for the ancients, food symbolized the parent images, outwardly projected to form the belief in protective gods and goddesses who not only controlled the fertility of the crops, but who were actually believed to live within the growing vegetation. These ideas were rational in that they expressed early man's awareness of the vital powers of nature which are manifested in healthy human life; irrational in that they expressed infantile dependency and libidinal ties to the parental images. Malinowski wrote:

> To primitive man, never, even under the best conditions, quite free from the threat of starvation, abundance of food is a

primary condition of normal life. It means the possibility of looking beyond the daily worries, of paying more attention to the remoter, spiritual aspects of civilization. If we thus consider that food is the main link between man and his surroundings, that by receiving it he feels the forces of destiny and providence, we can see the cultural, nay, biological importance of primitive religion in the sacralization of food. We can see in it the germs of what in higher types of religion will develop into the feeling of dependence upon Providence, of gratitude, and of confidence in it.[1]

2. THE MOTHER IMAGE
IN PRIMITIVE COSMOLOGY

The cult of the Earth Mother as the creative power in nature is found in primitive societies in many parts of the world, and underlies the religions of the higher cultures. Our term "Mother Nature" is a survival of this archaic mode of thought. Indeed, survivals of the mother cult in peasant life and in mythology exist to this day as submerged and almost forgotten segments of the traditions of our culture. The worship of the Mother Goddess can be traced back to paleolithic times, preceding the advent of agriculture,[2] and it has even been suggested that agriculture and the domestication of animals originated in the veneration of the maternal deity.

The Romans, as well as the Greeks and Minoans, personified and worshiped the Earth as a Mother Goddess. Sacrifices were made to her, and she was often invoked in the taking of oaths of loyalty. Part of the veneration of the Earth Goddess, the source of all life, consisted of the bringing of votive offerings to her shrine. The number of votaries of the Ephesian Artemis, for example, was enormous, and her temple was continually visited by hordes of pilgrims bringing dedicatory gifts.[3]

The Greek Artemis and Diana, both mother goddesses, personified the vegetable and animal life in nature. At Dodona, Delphi, and Olympia, three of the most important cult centers of ancient Greece, the worship of the Earth Goddess existed from great antiquity; and altars and sanctuaries of Earth were present in many of the Greek cities, such as Agae in Achaia, where she possessed the title of "broad-bosomed." One of the Homeric hymns, entitled "Earth, the Mother of All," runs:

I'll sing of Earth, Mother of All, of her the firm-founded,
Eldest of beings, her who feeds all that in the world exists;
All things that go upon the sacred land and on the sea,
And all that fly, all they are fed from thy bounty.
By thee, O Queen, are men blessed in their children,
   blessed in their crops;
Thine it is to give life and to take it back
From mortal men. Happy is he whom thou in heart
Dost honor graciously; he hath all things in plenty. . . .
Such are they whom thou dost honor, Goddess revered,
O bounteous Spirit.
Hail, Mother of Gods, Spouse of the Starry Sky,
And graciously for this my song bestow on me
Substance enough for heart's ease. So shall I not forget
To hymn thee in another lay.[4]

The creative powers of the maternal deity were believed to be manifested in the fertility of the crops, and in many instances the Earth Goddess represented the food supply. In ancient Greece, the goddesses Demeter and Persephone embodied the corn, and often appeared in ancient art wearing and carrying stalks of corn. A coin of the fourth century B.C.[5] shows the goddess in the earth, immersed in the growing corn. She does not simply make the corn grow; she *is* the corn itself.

A great number of customs paralleling the Corn Mother and Barley Mother of ancient Greece have been collected from modern European folklore, and numerous analogies can be found in the rituals of the Rice Mother in the East Indies.

3. THE ANIMAL DEITY AS MOTHER IMAGE

The worship of animal deities was prevalent throughout ancient religion, and the fertility goddess often appeared in the form of an animal. This veneration of animals, psychoanalytic studies indicate, resulted from the projection of the parent-child relationship to the animal. In modern animal phobias, for example, the fear of the animal is basically a fear of the father, and our affection for pets is to a large extent based on the transference of familial feelings.

Many ancient divinities, particuarly the goddesses, appeared in the form of animals, and the frequent metamorphosis of the heroes in Greek and Roman mythology into animal shape, and vice versa, is indicative of this ancient theriomorphism.[6] In primitive belief, the growing crops are often embodied by animals—for example, the corn spirit has taken such diverse animal forms as the wolf, dog, hare, fox, cock, goose, quail, cat, goat, cow, bull, pig, and horse, in various cultures.

The snake was a symbol of the mother fertility goddess, and the familiar serpent of Athena seems to have been a representation of an ancient earth goddess whose worship was later synthesized with that of Athena.[7] Athena herself is frequently referred to in Homer as "cow-eyed," and was probably worshiped in the form of a cow, for the Mycenaeans, the predecessors of the Greeks, worshiped a cow goddess. Aphrodite was venerated in the form of a horse, and the goddess Hekate assumed the shape of a dog.

In some instances, the animal goddess seems to have been eaten in a sacrificial communion meal. Evidence indicates, for example, that at the Greek Thesmophoria festival the women ate swine's flesh in a ritual repast, and that a holy meal of swine formed part of the worship of Adonis and the mother goddess Aphrodite. The goat, often a sacrificial animal in ancient times, represented Amalthea or Rhea, the fertility goddesses who were the mothers of Zeus. Artemis, an early fertility spirit, was worshiped as a bull goddess. This maternal deity was also venerated in the form of a bear, her priestesses, clad in bear-skins, dancing around her animal representation to identify themselves with the goddess.*

Thus, animals that in myth or in artistic form were regarded as "attributes of" or "sacred to" a goddess were originally animal personifications of the goddess herself. For example, the pig was regarded as "sacred to" Demeter; pigs were sacrificed in her rituals, and she was frequently portrayed carrying or being accompanied by a pig. The close association between deity and animal was common throughout ancient Greek culture, and numerous art forms depict humans with animal heads, representing deities. Goddesses were often portrayed with the heads of cows, and gods with the heads of bulls.

4. PATERNAL DEITIES
AND THE FOOD SUPPLY

Just as the maternal image was projected into nature in primitive cosmology, so the father figure was the basis for the paternal deities.

The conception of the divine in terms of the paternal image is not a type of infantilism, as Freud thought; on the contrary, the belief in a cosmic providence may stem from a deep inner security developed from a healthy relation with the father. Religion is valid if it represents an individual's identification with the creative powers in nature. Freud's viewpoint was that early man, feeling himself helpless and weak in the midst of powerful natural forces, projected into the cosmos his childhood image of an all-powerful protecting father, in order to obtain

---

* The goddess Nemesis, whose name later came to mean "distribution,"[8] was early identified with Artemis. Themis, the goddess of justice, was originally identified with Ge, an earth goddess.[9]

relief and comfort in the face of the menacing powers of nature. In other words, natural forces could be controlled by communing with a father who, it was believed, controlled the universe.

There is no doubt that the father as the provider of food becomes intimately associated and identified with creativity and protection. In a primitive culture, particularly, as the child becomes older, the father is more and more regarded as the source of food, and his authority tends to become invariably connected with his role as distributor of nourishment. According to Richards, the whole structure of government in the Bantu tribes is built upon this attitude toward filial authority.[10]

The close connection between the father image and the food supply explains the significance of many primitive agricultural rites, for much of early myth and ritual was concerned with magical methods for obtaining a good harvest. Throughout primitive religion, we find innumerable rites to placate, propitiate, and to exhort the deity to provide a good harvest. In fact, the sacrificial systems of the ancient peoples largely consisted of the offering of gifts to the divine powers to insure an abundance of food. Rain magic and seasonal ceremonies are well-known illustrations of these practices. Father Zeus himself was a rain god, and in times of drought the Athenians besought him to rain on the cornland by sacrificing at his altars.[11]

5. THE FATHER IMAGE
AS FERTILITY SPIRIT

The tendency of the immature mind to overestimate the powers of the father explains in part the phenomenon of the magician-king found in numerous primitive cultures. In many instances, the position of the king arose out of that of the tribal magician, who controlled the forces of nature for the welfare of the community.[12] The most important need of the group was a plentiful supply of food; for this reason the main efforts of the magician-king were exerted to insure a good harvest. The rain-maker was a typical example of tribal magician. This authority-figure originated simply as the father, who as provider directed the work efforts of the group toward obtaining a supply of food. With the extension of the family principle into larger social groups, the attitude toward the father was transferred to the priestly kings who were the rulers of the early city-states.[13]

The magician-king was often identified with the god. The belief in the divinity of royalty is frequently found in primitive societies; in fact, in many of the cultures of antiquity, as well as in China, Mexico, and Peru, the king himself *was* the deity. The early Babylonian kings claimed to be gods during their lifetimes; in the fourth dynasty of Ur, the kings had temples built for their worship, and the people were commanded to sacrifice to their statues. The kings of Egypt, as well, were deified during their lifetimes and were venerated in temples, where offerings were made at their altars.

Many of the early gods were identified with the powers of fertility and were believed to be incarnate in human kings who personified the vegetation spirit in religious ritual. The gods Osiris, Tammuz, Adonis, and Attis represented the annual decay and revival of the crops in various lands around the eastern Mediterranean, and were personified by the king in the sacred rites.

Festivals commemorating the death and resurrection of Attis were held in Rome and elsewhere at the time of the vernal equinox. Attis, whose name simply means "father," was identified with the corn; the goddess Cybele, his mother and lover, was also venerated as a fertility spirit, and was closely associated with him in ritual and myth. Tammuz, or Adonis (meaning "lord"), was worshiped as a vegetation deity, and was the lover of Ishtar, the great mother goddess who embodied the reproductive powers of nature. Similarly, Osiris, who was personified in religious ritual by the king of Egypt, was a corn god closely associated with Isis, a maternal goddess of the vegetation.

These gods were often represented by animals identified with the fertility spirit. Attis and Adonis, for example, were embodied in the pig, and Osiris was personified both as a pig and a bull. In early Greece, Poseidon was a horse god and Apollo a wolf god. Apparently the woodpecker in primitive Italy was an embodiment of the magician-king. There are also traces of the marriage of the king and queen, a ritual designed to influence representation of vegetation deities in animal form in the sacred magically the powers of vegetation.[14]

6. GROUP PSYCHOLOGY AND
THE ANIMAL SACRIFICE

Group psychology in the primitive Graeco-Roman civilization was largely centered around the magical worship of the fertility spirits, who were in the main outward projections of the parental images. The earliest groups were for the most part based upon mutual identification with a common mother. In primitive Greek culture, all of the institutions on which the household and state depended were associated with the name and the cult of the corn goddess; the mother image was thus at the core of the social organization of the first cities. The Asiatic Artemis, for example, was the state goddess of the most ancient cities in Euboea, Chalcis, and Eretria.[15] The Greek city had as its focal point the shrine of the city goddess: the temple of Athena was the center of Athenian culture, as was the temple of Aphrodite at Corinth. In some instances these temples and their goddess can be directly traced back to the sanctuaries of the great mother goddesses of fertility.[16]

The fertility spirit, in animal form, was often the sacrificial victim in the ritual meals which were at the center of the social organization of the ancient cities. The holy repast was an occasion at which each communicant reidentified himself with the divinity. "If we turn now to the records of animal sacrifice in the various states of Greece," Farnell wrote, "we discern clearly that the victim was often regarded as the temporary incarnation of the deity, and if in this case it was eaten by the worshipers, we must interpret this as a mystic ceremony of communion with the godhead."[17]

Rites of this type are common among primitives all over the world, the most often encountered ceremony being the drinking of the blood of a sacrificial victim to establish a blood brotherhood. The act of communion with the same divinity establishes a bond of loyalty among the members of the cult group. The eating of bread together, frequently in animal or human form, is a well-known example of this practice. Thurnwald states that bread is sanctified in most agricultural communities, and is often regarded as the bearer, in concentrated form, of the vital powers of the cosmos.[18] The killing and sacramental eating of the body of the corn spirit, or of bread made in his or her image, is a frequently found practice in early cultures.

The sacrifice at the altar, an essential part of all religions, thus originally had a different significance than the later conception of a propitiatory offering or a plea for favor. The animal sacrifice was a public ritual, a social and religious obligation requiring all members of the group to join in this repast of worshipers with the god. The time of the sacrificial feast was a holy day, an occasion for renouncing self-interest, enthusiastically affirming the common welfare, and for holding communion with the deity.

The sacred meal was hence an event of the highest ethical importance, and was based upon certain primitive conceptions about eating and drinking in common. To eat and drink with another person was to establish a mutual bond of obligation between both individuals, i.e., to bring about a covenant (contract) between the communicants. The sacrificial repast expressed the fact that the god and his worshipers were bound together by holy and immutable ties of loyalty and duty.

Originally, a community of individuals worshiping the same god and sharing the same social duties was simply the kinship group, and the god himself was regarded as a member of the community. The common meal was therefore an occasion when the kinsmen met to seal and renew their feeling of brotherhood. In early times, the one unconditional, eternal bond which existed was that of kinship, which signified being part of a common substance. For example, the Hebrew phrase which expresses kinship is "Thou art my bone and my flesh." This belief is based on the fact that all of the kin have sprung from the mother's body, and have been nourished by her milk. Participation in a common meal thus engendered the belief that a kinship bond was either being established or reaffirmed. When a person shared a meal with his god, the conviction was expressed that both the divinity and the worshiper were part of a common substance, and hence were mutually bound together by loyalty; strangers were not permitted to participate in the common meals. The divine animal was regarded as one of the kinsmen,* and in mutually partaking of its flesh and blood the members of the community renewed their identification with each other and with their god.

These beliefs existed in sacrificial customs throughout the world of antiquity. The bond among the citizens of the ancient city was the life of the divine sacrificial animal whose flesh and blood were shared by the communicants in the sacred ritual presided over by the priestly king.

---

* Robertson Smith's theory that the sacrificial animal was the totem[19] will be discussed in a later chapter.

seven

RELIGIOUS RELICS
AND DIVINE
IDENTIFICATION

1. THE BELIEF IN MAGIC

Money takes many forms in modern life, for this institution is the result of the interplay of human beings continually entering into new relationships for fulfilling each other's needs. The diversity of human relationships which come into existence creates a corresponding multiplicity of symbolisms, all of which we are accustomed to call "money." Accounts receivable are money, marketable securities are money, accrued interest charges are money. So are mortgages, pawnbrokers' tickets, stock warrants, and letters of credit.

These are a few of the innumerable symbolic forms that money takes in our society; and to most of us, dependent as we are upon these symbols for our security and self-fulfillment, nothing sounds more like the very bedrock of reality than to say that we are "getting down to business." But is a contract to buy wheat that has not yet been planted a reality? Is the balance sheet item "Goodwill" a substantial entity? We may even question whether factories and inventories are actualities, for without people to work and to consume, these economic goods are material objects devoid of significance.

The fact is that the symbols and practices upon which business is ultimately based are in reality human attitudes and emotions operating within social institutions which seem real to us only because they are so familiar. What appears to us to be the soundest, most natural of practices may, from a detached, anthropological viewpoint, be as odd and as irrational as many of the primitive beliefs and customs we have been considering. The great depression of the 1930's, in which millions of men, dispirited, lived in the midst of a vast technological capacity without adequate food, heat, medical attention, and the opportunity for productive work, might well seem as weird and as cruel to an objective observer as the ancient custom of sacrificing humans for the good of the crops.

The true reality is man's creative will, expressing itself in work and love, and manifesting itself in diverse ways in myriad institutional settings. Indeed, there is a growing tendency among some economists to conceive of money as simply a reckoning device, or unit of calculation, which enables records to be kept of each person's ownership of present and future wealth, along with a history of all past activities relating to these records. But many of us still cling to what some economists have called "the gold-standard fetish," the belief that a sound monetary system must be based upon the convertibility of all money, if the owner so wishes, into gold.

Such an outlook fails to place money within the context of an entire culture, as an institution which can be modified and reconstituted so as to promote creativity and happiness for all people. To grasp the frame of mind which produced such beliefs as the fetishism of gold, we must turn back through the centuries to a mentality which has now become foreign and strange to us. We must imagine a magical world view in which astrology existed rather than astronomy, alchemy rather than chemistry, and number mysticism rather than mathematics.

The belief in imitative and contagious magic exists in all primitive cultures, and ancient Greece and Rome were suffused with such ideas and practices. A well-known example of imitative magic is the attempt to inflict harm upon an enemy by injuring or destroying his image. The sorcerer believes that by drawing a picture of a person on the ground, and then striking or otherwise harming the picture, the individual will be injured in a corresponding manner. The way in which the image is disfigured or struck determines the way in which the actual person is to be affected. Idol worship, fetishism, and the belief in talismans stem from these conceptions.

Contagious magic rests upon the belief that objects which have once been in contact with one another retain, even when separated, a mystic connection or sympathy. For this reason, distant objects are sometimes regarded as bound together in an occult unity. A mystic bond is also believed to exist between a person and any severed part of his body, such as his hair, nails, teeth, spittle, or excrement. An inner sympathy is present between an individual and his footprints, as well as between a wound and the weapon which caused the injury.

In many regions, an occult connection is believed to exist between a person and his spilled blood, as well as between himself and his clothing. Any injury done to a man's clothing is also inflicted upon that person. Indeed, any impression made by the body retains a mystic connection with the individual. The aborigines of southeastern Australia, for example, believe that man can be harmed if someone sticks sharp pieces of

quartz or glass into the marks made in the earth by his re-
clining body.

2. THE CAUSATION OF MAGIC

Magic is to a large extent based upon a mistaken application
of the association of ideas within the mind and in communication. Men believed that the control which they exerted over
their inner ideas enabled them to exercise a similar control over
the external world.[1] Primitive man projects into the outer world
the processes by which the mind utilizes symbols, failing to
distinguish between these images and the reality from which
they were originally drawn.

This type of thinking is a characteristic of the child mentality.
According to psychoanalytic theory, magic is an infantile manifestation closely associated with the oral, nondifferentiated stage
in which the child regards itself as omnipotent.[2] The primitive
mind allows the desires which produce imaginative constructions
to triumph over the actualities of the external world. The child's
dependency upon the mother for food, expressed primarily in
suckling, tends to be transferred into the cosmos by primitives,
producing the belief in mother goddesses who provide nourishment and magical aid.[3]

We should not, of course, regard early man as completely
dominated by fantasy. The primitive carries out his technical
activities in an efficient manner, based on a large body of
everyday practical observations. At the same time, however, he
clings to magical ceremonies and rituals to facilitate and render
possible his technological operations.[4]

The psychological truth behind the belief that the divine
powers can be influenced by sacrificial offerings is that these
prayers are in reality inward creative dedications. The primitive
priest, lacking a philosophy to explain the real and profound
experiences he may undergo, must call upon symbols of an
irrational nature to interpret these experiences. As Dawson

says,[5] this does not make the experience less real or irrational; it is merely that the system which he builds up to express his insights is crude and superstitious. Thus, at the core of primitive religion, despite its many magical, almost psychotic rituals, there existed a powerful emotional affirmation of the creative powers of nature.

3. RITUAL CANNIBALISM

Among primitives all over the world, the act of eating is closely associated with contagious magic; in eating an object the primitive believes that he thereby acquires the object's qualities.[6] Some North American tribes, for instance, believed that a person who eats deer meat becomes a faster runner and a more clever thinker than a man who partakes of the flesh of awkward animals such as bears or swine. The Caribs, to take another example, refused to eat swine for fear that they would acquire the small eyes of pigs.

By eating the body of a person, the primitive therefore believes that he obtains the characteristics of that individual. Many practices illustrate this magical belief, such as the widespread custom in which savages eat the flesh and drink the blood of a brave man in order to obtain his courage.

The magical aspects of cannibalism have their counterpart in the infantile stage in which the child regards itself as part of the maternal body: in feeding at the breast, the infant identifies itself with the mother. This phenomenon is well-known to psychoanalysts, who have found that the child may be ambivalent in its cannibalistic desires, wishing both to possess and identify with the loved mother, and to injure and destroy her at the same time.

The fertility spirit eaten in ritual was sometimes embodied in human form; and the sacrificial repast in these instances was in the nature of a cannibalistic feast, in which a member of the group, occasionally the king, was ceremonially devoured.

Ritual cannibalism is frequently found in primitive cultures. Among the Kwakiutl, for example, one of the highest honors an individual could attain was to be initiated into the Cannibal Society, admission into which required that the neophyte eat the entire corpse of a deceased relative. Similar phenomena have been found in parts of Africa.[7] Numerous myths and rituals attest to the existence of cannibalism in ancient Greece and Rome, as, for instance, the story of the eating of Pelops, the legend of the human sacrifices offered to Zeus Lycaeus, and the myth of Dionysus eaten by the Titans. Scholars are of the opinion that human flesh was sporadically eaten in religious ceremonies in Greece as late as the Roman period.[8]

Disgusting and gruesome as these practices may seem to us, they had a higher, as well as a perverse significance for primitive men. Thus, in New Guinea, devouring the dead, while enacted with nausea and dread, was at the same time a sacred duty expressing affection and respect.[9] Cannibalism often served as an expression of love and honor for the departed kinsman, or as a means of establishing a communion or blood covenant with the dead.[10] Eating the king enabled his subjects to acquire magically his divine powers. According to some ancient authorities, Romulus was killed, and each senator carried away a portion of his flesh under his garments. A possible parallel to this occurrence is the cutting up of the dead body of Halfdan, a king of Norway, after which every district in the kingdom sought to obtain a portion of the corpse, in order to acquire the ruler's supernatural energies.[11]

4. THE MAGIC OF RELICS

The worship of the sacred relic stemmed from practices and beliefs which were either directly or symbolically cannibalistic, as is attested by innumerable instances in primitive cultures in which the bones, skin, blood, flesh, or skull of a deceased person are regarded as talismans. Through contagious magic, possession of a relic enables the individual to acquire for himself the qualities of its original owner; and, when the dead person is believed to have been divine or holy, the possession of this sacred object makes it possible for its owner to identify himself with the deity.

The widespread veneration of relics and the use made of their marvelous powers was part of the ancestral cults of antiquity, for the sacred objects associated with the dead heroes were worshiped with the same feelings as the ancestors themselves.[12] Possession of the relics of the hero was believed to be vital to the safety of the city: they made the fields fertile and the crops abundant, and prevented famine, pestilence, or drought. These magic mementos also possessed healing powers and other wondrous virtues. Not only the bones of the heroes, but also other property of the honored dead were enshrined and venerated. The spear of Achilles was preserved in the temple of Athena at Phaselis, the sword of Memnon in the temple of Aesculapius, and the shield of Pyrrhus in the sanctuary of Demeter. The lyre of Orpheus, the flute of Marsyas, the scepter of Agamemnon, and the sandals of Helen were other sacred objects that were preserved and honored.

From the earliest times, relics were carried as amulets, which enabled a person to obtain the healing and protective powers of the hero to whom they had belonged. They were placed on the handles of weapons and in the crowns and regalia of kings. Similar beliefs survive to this day in the form of lucky charms and good-luck pieces, many of which, by the way, are not unlike coins in shape and design.

It was held that the welfare of the city depended upon the preservation of the bones and relics of its kings, and that the loss or destruction of these sacred objects would bring disaster upon the community. For this reason, when an ancient city was conquered, it was not merely an insulting gesture when the victor violated the tomb of the city's past kings; this act was a powerful blow against the kingdom.[13] The bones of the kings of Elam were carried off to Assyria by Assurbanipal for this reason. To achieve the same result, the bones of the king of Edom were burned into lime by the Moabites. Similarly, Lysimachus is reputed to have scattered the bones of the dead kings of Epirus after opening their graves.

Early statues were akin to relics in that they were idols, images possessing magical powers. The statue of a god *was* the god, and was often worshiped as a deity. For this reason, statues were believed to protect the city, and offerings and sacrifices were made to them.

> Among primitive peoples there is a belief in a near connexion between an image and the person or thing portrayed; so that what affects the image must also affect the original of the image. Connected with beliefs of this kind were some of the customs of early Greek religion. The temple was the abode of the deity, his image being his surrogate, and taking his place. The deity in a measure resided in the image; petitions to him were laid on its knees, incense was burned before it, and the treasures given to the god were heaped about it. Among the most pleasing gifts to the god were other images, whether of himself or of votaries.[14]

5. THE REGALIA OF THE KING

Because of the belief in magic, the king's body and his property, indeed anything associated with him, was felt to participate in his godlike potencies. All of his actions were surrounded by his *mana*—a mysterious charge, as it were, possessed by this divine person, which spread by a mystic contagion into anything in any way connected with him. This belief in the magic powers of royalty persisted in Europe until relatively modern times. It was believed, for example, that the English kings could heal scrofula by their touch. Queen Elizabeth often exercised this miraculous gift, and in 1633 Charles the First cured a hundred patients through his magic powers. Survivals of these ideas exist today in the awe in which celebrities are held, as illustrated in such practices as autograph hunting.

The royal regalia, one of the oldest types of political symbols, originated in the king's relics. These symbols of the primitive kingship often consist of portions of the body of deceased rulers, which are enshrined as sacred objects. Among certain tribes of southern Madagascar, a neck bone, a nail, and a lock of hair of a deceased king are kept along with the similar relics of his predecessors, and constitute the right to the kingship.[15]

In some instances, the new king is required to eat part of his dead predecessor in order to acquire his virtues. At Abeokuta the head of the preceding monarch was given to the new sovereign, who was obliged to eat the old king's tongue. Similarly, at Ibadan in West Africa, the heart of the deceased king was eaten by his successor. In southern Celebes, the regalia are fetishes or heirlooms that confer title to the kingship, and that serve as public amulets and instruments of divination. The holiest regalia consist of relics of the bodies of dead royalty.

6. THE HIGHER SYMBOLISM OF RELICS

In its infantile aspect, the relic was akin to a psychopathic fetish, in that it was a morbid object representing an oral fixation upon an early libidinal object choice. In this sense, the loathsome practices recounted above were expressions of emotional attachments to parent images, manifested by archaic modes of magical identification. Mourning a lost love object, Freud stated,[16] is often accompanied by the introjection of that object into the ego: the cannibal, like the infant, carries out this identification literally, through oral incorporation. The relic, in its form as an amulet, may be said to have expressed a childlike effort to obtain omnipotence by magically acquiring the miraculous powers of the overvalued parent.

The loftier feelings associated with the cult of relics stemmed from the same motivations as were present in ancestor worship— the need to become identified with the sacred tradition embodied by the heroic dead.

The relic is an objectification of the memories of past emotional relationships with deceased individuals; it is a symbol of the soul of the dead. We discern in the relic the origin of the souvenir, a treasured remembrance of past times. This holy object symbolized for the ancient man a deep stratum of his emotional life—memories of old loves, grief toward the loss of these loved ones, and inspiration for present devotion drawn from the past. The relic was a family remembrance, an heirloom, the symbol of a deceased ancestral hero, whose beloved memory served to exemplify the divine spirit with which each person sought to identify himself. It was a sacred souvenir, like the *churinga* of the primitive Australian, the center of the tradition and the bonds of loyalty among the members of the kinship group. The various objects associated with a hero tend to become symbols of his great deeds and virtues. If the sign is not confused with its referent, as in magic, this is a normal psychological process.* The regalia in their rational aspect are monuments, or memorials. These symbols serve as a constant source of inspiration for other individuals to perpetuate the tradition represented by the noble men of the past: they are symbols of the soul of the hero.

7. RING MONEY AND RELICS

Many practices illustrating the normal symbolism of relics are to be found in everyday modern life, as for example the lock of hair or the photograph of a sweetheart carried by a lover. The wedding ring, too, expresses affection, devotion, and loving communion between husband and wife.

Political loyalties and friendships, as well as remembrances

---

* The bones of the founder of the American Navy, John Paul Jones, were brought back from France after his death to be placed beneath the dome at Annapolis. His tomb bears the inscription:

JOHN PAUL JONES
HE GAVE OUR NAVY ITS EARLIEST TRADITIONS
OF HEROISM AND VICTORY

of public honor, are also frequently expressed in souvenirs, memorials, or monuments. For example, it is customary for members of the United States Cabinet to take their chairs with them upon retiring from their position at the White House. Rings have possessed similar symbolic meanings throughout history. George Washington, for instance, made a gift of a ring with a lock of his hair placed beneath a glass.[17] It was, in fact, a common practice in the past for kings to distribute rings as tokens of gratitude or favor.

Rings have been used as amulets from the earliest times, their magical significance resulting partly from primitive beliefs about circles, which were supposed to embody such qualities as perfection and eternity. Rings were believed to establish unbreakable bonds of love among their wearers, and were often treasured heirlooms representing the family tradition. These ornaments were frequently regarded as amulets containing the special powers of their original owners.

The signet ring was widely employed as a magical charm in in ancient times, and possessed the added magical value of bearing a sacred image. Indeed, there is reason to believe that bracelets, anklets, and girdles were originally amulets which later became ornaments. Bracelets were emblems of kingship in the East; they were worn by the kings of Persia, and formed part of the regalia of the biblical King Saul. Rings have been worn almost universally. Their use as a royal ornament in ancient times is attested to by the myths surrounding the rings of Nestor, Minos, and of Polycrates, tyrant of Samos. The gold ring was frequently bestowed as a military honor in ancient Rome, and the emperor's ring was a type of state seal.[18]

Ring money was in widespread use in prehistoric times, and its presence in many primitive communities is well-known to anthropologists. Rings were used as money in early Egypt, and have been found in the treasuries of Mycenae and Knossus in Crete. Ancient German mythology and prehistoric findings throughout Europe and the Near East give evidence that rings were used for payments of various types.[19]

It would appear that ancient ring money was a form of religious remembrance, possessing magical potencies and symbolizing devotion to the tradition embodied by the king. Ancient coinage, as we shall see, had a similar origin. However, before continuing the story of how ancient money evolved, as a sacred relic, from the sacrificial feast, we must pursue further the regalia and their significance in the social organizations of antiquity.

eight

THE STRUGGLE
FOR POWER

1. THE IRRATIONAL DRIVE FOR MONEY

A conflict as grim and in its own way as savage as any barbaric ritual is regularly enacted every day in thousands of offices, bureaus, shops, and factories throughout the world. This is the struggle for omnipotence. It may take place among the lowest paid of clerks or manual workers, in the top echelons of a giant corporation, in the halls of a famous university, in a woman's club, or in the innermost caucuses of a political party, for there is no place, no institution, no sanctum where this struggle may not occur. Even the disciples of Christ, we are told, had their rivalries.

In its rawest aspect, we can conceive of the common meal as a physical brawl, each participant grabbing, pushing, and shoving to get a portion of food, in a manner analogous to the scrambling for jobs which sometimes occurs in modern organizations. The "love feast" may often have been dominated by a bully, and at its worst may have been a struggle for food in which the strongest survived and the weakest died of starvation. We tend to forget that most of our meals are obtained by killing other animals or vegetation. Although mutual aid and cooperation are frequently observed among wild beasts, and are an important factor in the survival of species, the life and death struggle is nevertheless an everyday occurrence among animals in their natural habitats, the loser often serving as the victor's repast. The fight for food can even be observed among animals nursing at the maternal breast. If there are not enough nipples for an entire brood of kittens, for example, a puny cat tends to be deprived of its mother's milk by its more vigorous siblings. Among primitive human groups, parents are often killed, or are expected to commit suicide, when they become too old to assist in the quest for food.

It is a rational part of human nature for individuals to seek to actualize their intellectual and emotional powers by seeking social positions which will enable them to exercise their creative capacities to a greater degree. Very likely an element of inevitable tragedy is inherent in human life, in that all of the aspirants for a particular position in a social group are not qualified to succeed in their goals. It is a mark of maturity when an individual is capable of accepting emotionally such frustrations to his goals.

But what is irrational in human nature is the quest for undeserved position within the division of labor, and this infantile desire to be all-powerful is the source of much injustice. Insofar as money expresses this irrational motivation within us, it is indeed the root of all evil.

The king, as priest, magistrate, and distributor of food, was the economic administrator in ancient times, and for this reason his image was often placed on ancient coins. The classic symbols of his regal authority—the crown, the scepter, and the eagle—which to this day survive as heraldic decorations on our coinage, originated as relics, or regalia, and expressed, like the common meal, both the moral and immature aspects of early group psychology.

The management of the domestic economy was carried out by the imposition of instinctual renunciations on the members of the group by the king. Ideally, this allotment of tasks and the distribution of food and other goods was accepted in a devoted fashion. In actual practice, however, this love must often have been intermixed with ambivalence. The hubris of the king or subject may have caused antagonism, and under primitive conditions, this hostility often erupted into physical violence. The regalia and the animal sacrifice, as we will now show, symbolized not only the majesty of the sacred tradition, but also a raw struggle for power centering around the succession to the kingship.

2. THE REGALIA AND THE SACRED TREE

The regalia can be traced back to tree worship, a practice which was widespread in ancient Greece and Italy, as well as in Crete and in the Mycenaean world.[1] According to Tylor, holy groves or trees were among the first places of religious worship.[2] The first temples were clearings in the primeval forest, and were comprised of a few trees upon which the devotees hung the skins of sacrificial victims. In early Greece, the priest of the grove would offer sacrifices to Zeus at the base of a holy tree: this was the origin of the rituals of the temple worship.[3] Throughout the writings of Pausanias, Strabo, and Pliny, as well as Homer, there are numerous references to sacrificial feasts held in holy groves.

The first temples were thus sacred trees, within which the deity was believed to live, expressing his will through signs and oracles.[4] At Dodona, perhaps the oldest of all Greek sanctuaries,

Zeus was believed to live within a sacred tree, and in ancient
Rome Jupiter was originally venerated in the form of a great
oak tree which grew upon the Capitol.[5]

The kings of Rome, personifying Jupiter, appeared in state
processions with a scepter adorned with an eagle, and wearing a
gold crown fashioned in the form of leaves. All of the Greek
kings also carried a scepter, for this staff of office inspired the
ruler with knowledge of the *themistes,* the infallible laws handed
down by sacred tradition, which enabled them to execute the will
of the god within the domestic group. The scepter of the
priestly king, originating in the branch of the sacred tree,[6] was
in a sense a magician's wand,[7] for the holy tree, as an embodiment of the divine ruler, possessed his magical powers to control natural occurrences. There is reason to believe that the priest
of Zeus Lykaios made rain magic with an oak branch.

The king's crown, as is obvious, also originated in the magical
veneration of a sacred tree. The wearing of the crown was taken
as evidence that an individual had entered into the deepest
possible communion with the deity, and it was unthinkable for
a person to preside at a religious ritual without bearing this
symbol.

The eagle, which appears on many of our coins, and which
surmounts the American flag much as it did the scepter of the
Roman king, seems to have been at first an image of the ruler.
In early bird cults, the sacred bird was identified with the
magician-king. Among the Greeks and Romans the study of birds
was basic to the mantic art: birds were not merely portents, but
were agents controlling the weather. Indeed, the soul of the king
was believed to appear in the form of an eagle, in this way
watching over his people and his domains.[8] The eagle was an
animal embodiment of Zeus.

3. KILLING THE VEGETATION SPIRIT

Ritual regicide was a recurrent theme in early times. Kings
were killed upon the challenge of a new contender for the office,

or at the termination of some seasonal or vegetation cycle.*
During this period of time, the king controlled, indeed embodied,
the fertility of the calendar period. Where the length of office
was determined by the completion of the earth's solar revolution,
the struggle for the kingship often took the mythological form
of the dying out of the old year and the appearance of the
vigorous new spirit of the coming period.

---

* Frazer's hypotheses concerning the rites at Nemi have been rejected
by most classical scholars. According to his interpretation, at the Arician
grove at Nemi, sacred to Diana of the Wood, it was necessary to kill the
existing King of the Wood in order to succeed to the king-priesthood and
mate with the mother goddess. However, a preliminary ritual had to be
performed before the aspirant could legitimately fight the ruling king:
There grew within the grove at Nemi a sacred oak tree embodying Jupiter
(Zeus). It was forbidden to break a holy branch off this tree, but once
having succeeded in doing so, a person was eligible to challenge the King
of the Wood.

The holy grove at Nemi was of great antiquity, having existed prior
to 496 B.C., and there is reason to believe that it was a common place of
worship for many of the oldest cities, perhaps for the entire Latin confederacy. According to Frazer, there is reason to believe that the early kings
of Rome performed a similar function to the priestly king at Nemi—
reigning as gods, mating with a mother goddess, and proving their divine
status in a severe, often fatal, bodily struggle with an aspirant to the crown.

Frazer concluded that the holy bough on the sacred oak which had to
be broken off was in actuality a sprig of mistletoe.9 Mistletoe has been
regarded as possessing sacred potency from time immemorial among the
Indo-Europeans. This phallic symbol was the object of religious veneration, and was mystically linked with the vital powers of the sun. The
King of the Wood at Nemi personified the oak on which grew the mistletoe: the oak tree was magically identified with the body of the god. It
would appear that, to succeed to the priest-kingship, the aspirant had to
cut off part of the god's body; victory in this combat entitled the winner
to the love of Diana, the mother goddess.

It hardly requires a knowledge of Freudian theory to interpret the rule
of succession to the kingship at Nemi as based upon the castration of the
King of the Wood, who represented father Zeus. Similar struggles between
father and son are mirrored in Orphic theology. Cronus cut off the phallus
of his father Uranus, the sky god, while he was sleeping with the Earth
Goddess, thereby deposing him from the throne of heaven, and was in
turn castrated by his own offspring Zeus, who then succeeded to the
divine crown.

Frazer's work suggests that the holy fire, the focal point of the ancient
temple and one of the oldest and most important symbols of the perpetuity
of the state, had its origin in the worship of the oak. From the most distant
past, he said, the early Europeans have held fire festivals in which an im-

The killing of the ruler when his powers seemed to be waning
was perhaps not simply a matter of brutal calculation, but was
related to the belief in his divine capacities. For the king's life
was magically identified with the prosperity of the entire country,
so that if he became sick or impotent the crops would fail, the
cattle would die, and disease would become rampant.

The ritual murder of the king in his role as fertility spirit is
closely associated with the custom, found in many cultures, of
sacrificing humans to improve the harvest. In ancient Phrygia,
for example, the high priest was annually slain in the character
of Attis, a tree god, as an embodiment of the vegetation. In some
instances, because of its magical power, the flesh of the victim
played an important part in fertilizing the soil. In the annual
Osiris ritual, the victim, representing Osiris, was killed as a
personification of the corn spirit, and his ashes were scattered
over the fields to improve the fertility of the crops. In Chinna
Kimedy:

> The flesh cut from the victim was instantly taken home by
> the persons who had been deputed by each village to bring it
> . . . The bearer deposited it in the place of public assembly,
> where it was received by the priest and the heads of families.
> The priest divided it into two portions, one of which he offered
> to the Earth Goddess . . . The other portion of flesh he divided
> into as many shares as there were heads of houses present. Each
> head of a house rolled his shred of flesh in leaves, and buried it
> in his favorite field.[11]

There is a good deal of evidence that the sacrifice of the
fertility animal originated as the slaying of the king as vegetation spirit. When the ghastly ritual cited immediately above was
suppressed, it is known that an animal was often substituted for

---

portant part of the ritual consisted of burning a man representing the oak
god.

The cult of an oak Zeus, according to A. B. Cook,[10] was common
throughout Asia Minor, and at numerous cult centers Zeus dwelled in a
sacred oak and was served by a priest-king who reigned until slain by an
aspirant. At Olympia, at Cnossos, and probably at Dodona, the challenge
of the priestly king later gave rise to athletic contests. The Olympic games
may have originated in this fashion.

the human sacrifice; the flesh of the victim retained its magical power of fertility, and great haste and struggle ensued to obtain a portion to bury in the fields.

In numerous instances an animal is eaten as a substitute for the corpse of a dead kinsman. Sometimes an animal is brought into close contact with the corpse before being eaten. Hartland mentioned a case in which a goat, reared in the corpse's name, was sacrificed wearing his clothes.[12]

It seems likely that the custom of killing the king's son as a substitute for the king existed in ancient Greece, and that in later times an animal was used in place of the child victim. It was a common practice to substitute an animal for a human sacrifice. The bull was often chosen for this purpose, as in Borneo, where, after human sacrifice was abolished, various tribes kept cattle for the sole purpose of sacrificing them in the place of humans at mortuary rites and other ceremonies. In ancient times, a man was sacrificed each year at Salamis to Aphrodite, and later to Diomedes, but in the course of time an ox was substituted. The identification of the ruler of Crete with a bull god illustrates the substitution of an animal victim for the divine king. The ancient bull sacrifice expressed hostility toward the king,* the director of economic activity, and this ambivalence was symbolized by the imagery of the king and his regalia on the ancient coins.

---

* Survivals to this day of this manner of expressing hostility toward state authority exist in the modern Spanish bull fight.[13]

PART 4

The Origin of Money in
the Sacrificial Meal

nine

THE BULL GOD AS SACRIFICIAL ANIMAL

1. THE DIVINITY OF THE BULL

For some people, the quintessence of living is a juicy steak dinner at an expensive restaurant or night club. At these splendid dining establishments are often to be seen the richest, the best dressed, and the most famous of people, among them the idols of television, radio, stage, and movies. For it is not simply the delicious steak, but it is the *mana* of the distinguished clientele and the closeness to these celebrities which make the meal an occasion to be eagerly anticipated and remembered with pride. The magnificent décor adds to the feeling of being a member, so to speak, of the royal family, and the immaculate service lends a ceremonial, even ritual air to the entire evening.

Money as we know it today originated, in antiquity, in an institution similar to our modern steak dinner at a regal restaurant, namely in the communion meal of a sacrificial bull. The ritualistic killing and eating of a divine bull played an enormously important role in the sacrificial systems of ancient times, particularly in Greece and Rome; and it was from this institution that coinage later evolved.

The bull, symbolizing strength and heroism, was deified in most of the ancient Mediterranean cultures, being held as sacred in Egypt, Mesopotamia, Persia, Crete, and Greece, as well as India.

The identification of the king with the bull god was of very great significance in Egyptian religion. Texts refer to the king as a "strong bull," and the queen as mother of a son is called "the cow that hath borne a bull." The sun is called "the bull of heaven," and the sky itself is conceived as an enormous cow.

In Babylonia, tremendous statues of bulls guarded the entrances of buildings. These figures, frequently winged, possessed, in the Assyrian period, a human face, and sometimes were shown on gates or walls as attacking enemies. In the Epic of Gilgamesh, this animal, associated with the constellation Taurus, played a prominent role. The bull was the sacred animal of the god Hadad in northern Syria, and in Phoenicia it was associated with the deity Baal, the goddess Ishtar being represented by a cow.

The sacrifice of a bull god constituted the central ritual in the Mithraic religion, which as the official Roman cult flourished throughout the empire for many centuries.[1] In this ceremony, a bull decorated with flowers and gold leaf was driven on top of a grating over a pit, and was there gashed to death with a sacred spear. The hot, reeking blood of the animal poured down upon the worshiper, who let it drench his body completely. The neophyte emerged from the pit to receive the adoration and homage of the worshipers, as one who had been purified by the washing away of his sins. It is of interest that the testicles of the bull played an important part in the ritual. Mithraic mythology revolves about the slaying of a divine bull, and the presence of cornstalks issuing from the body of the dead animal in some of the cult monuments attests to its role as a vegetation spirit.

The Greek god Dionysus, who was frequently identified with Zeus, was often worshiped in the form of a bull, and there is reason to believe that in Athens every year the queen was ritually married to a bull representing this deity.

Dionysus was usually represented in the form of a bull, and was believed to appear in this shape. He was spoken of as "cowborn", "bull", "bull-shaped", "bull-faced", "bull-browed", "bull-horned", "bull-bearing", "two-horned", and "horned."[2] In artistic representations Dionysus was depicted as a bull or with bull horns. It is well known that Greek tragedy originated in a religious ritual in which a sacred bull (or goat) was killed and eaten in order that his *mana* might be distributed among the people.[3] The Argive Hera was called the "cow-headed" goddess, as was Athena; and the Cretan Zeus was venerated as a bull god. Thus,

> . . . the Cretans, when they acted the sufferings and death of Dionysus, tore a live bull to pieces with their teeth. Indeed, the rending and devouring of live bulls and calves appear to have been a regular feature of the Dionysiac rites. When we consider the practice of portraying the god as a bull or with some of the features of the animal, the belief that he appeared in bull form to his worshipers at the sacred rites, and the legend that in bull form he had been torn in pieces, we cannot doubt that in rending and devouring a live bull at his festival the worshipers of Dionysus believed themselves to be killing the god, eating his flesh, and drinking his blood.[4]

The bull was of tremendous significance in the Cretan culture, where it was a sacrificial animal identified both with the god and the king. In many works of art, the Minotaur is shown as a human figure with a horned bull-head, bovine ears, and tail, and it seems likely that the numerous rituals of the bull god in Crete originated in the practice of human sacrifice.[5]

A yearly offering of a bull to Zeus Sosipolis was made at the commencement of seed-time at Magnesia. In a solemn procession, headed by the priest and priestess, the bull was led to the sacrificial table, killed, and eaten in a communal meal in which his *mana* was distributed among the communicants. Artistic representations of the bull on the coins of Magnesia invariably show behind him an ear of grain, which attests that the animal was regarded as a fertility spirit. In a similar manner, at the Bouphonia, an Athenian ceremony, a divine bull was killed and eaten as a god of vegetation.

The relationship between the bull sacrifice, as an identification with the god, and the basis of ancient law and social organization, is clearly indicated in a blood covenant described by Plato in the *Critias*. According to this account, the laws of the island of Atlantis were inscribed on a pillar in the temple of Poseidon, where it was the custom for ten kings to hunt wild bulls which roamed freely within the sanctuary. When a bull was captured, it was brought to the pillar and its throat cut so that its blood would fall upon the holy inscriptions, whereupon each king cast a clot of the bull's blood in a bowl of wine, from which each drank to seal their oath of mutual loyalty.

The offering of bulls is frequently encountered in the writings of Homer, who speaks of the feast called the hekatomb, meaning literally 100 oxen. (Actually, the number of bulls in a hekatomb varied.) This pattern of ritual, well established centuries before Homeric times, was originally performed at rude, open altars, but in the course of the centuries magnificent temples, with hierarchies of priests and splendid processions, were the scene of these ceremonies. The early temple of Athena was called the Hekatompedon. Homer says of the sacrificial flesh that "each had his equal portion." The Bacchic initiate referred to the god Dionysus and Zagreus as "Him of the equal Feast." An inscription in Attica of approximately 330 B.C., however, contains a listing of the manner of distributing the bull's flesh, which seems to be proportionate to the status of the communicants:

> Five pieces each to the presidents
> Five pieces each to the nine archons

One piece each to the treasurers of the goddess
One piece each to the managers of the feast
The customary portions to others.[6]

2. RELICS OF THE SACRIFICIAL BULL

From the earliest times, the hearth has been associated with the mother image, Hestia. Round huts from the neolithic period have been found in Italian villages containing a hearth and a nearby pit filled with sacrificial remains.[7] Built of sacred stones, the hearth-altar may have been connected with the ancient pillar cult of the Mycenaean-Minoan period.

The sacrifice of the bull god was intimately associated with the sanctity of the altar, on which its blood, believed to possess a mystic potency, was poured. Apparently the skin of the sacrificed ox was also sacred, for it was worn by its worshipers. The "horns of consecration" found on Greek altars, consisting of a base with two erect horns bending outward at the tip, are a survival of the common ritual of placing the horns of the sacrificial bull before the cult image or upon the altar. In almost every sacred room excavated in Crete, as well as on every altar, the heads and horns of the bull are to be seen. The "horns of consecration" are also frequently found in close juxtaposition to the capitals of columns in architecture.

Through contagious magic, many of the ritual objects connected with the sacrifice of the bull shared in its *mana*, becoming magically imbued with its holiness. In the altar sacrifice, Farnell writes, "the whole process and the whole atmosphere seem to be charged with a perilous sanctity which attached to the sacrificer, the victim, special parts of the victim and especially his blood and his skin, and above all to the altar itself, the chief focus from which this 'mana' radiates upon every person and every thing that comes in contact with it."[8]

The killing and eating of the bull was for these reasons the source of certain relics which we may regard either as magical fetishes, or, in their higher symbolism, as religious souvenirs and memorials. The tripod, which was a unit of value in Homeric times, was traced by Sir Arthur Evans to an origin in the sacred pillar, upon which libations were poured. Apparently this object had a talismanic value, for Hylle, in Illyria, was guarded by a tripod buried beneath the city gates, and was thereby protected from hostile attacks. Similarly, the double axe, a well-known early religious cult symbol, appears to have originated as the weapon used for killing the sacrificial animal. The axe which the Tenedians used to sacrifice their victims was placed on their coins as an emblem of the city. Indeed, as we shall see, these relics of the bull sacrifice were the immediate predecessors of ancient coinage.

3. MODERN AFRICAN CATTLE CULTS

In order to broaden our perspective on the sociological significance of the bull cults of antiquity, it will be fruitful at this point to dwell briefly upon certain interesting parallels between the sacred cattle of early Crete, Greece, and Rome and the veneration of cattle in some modern African cultures.* The many comparable aspects of these contemporary practices to the bull worship of early Egypt have been discussed by Professor Frankfort.[9]

The most outstanding cultural trait in certain regions of Africa at the present time, according to Herskovits,[10] is the sacrosanct character of cattle. The Hamites and the half-Hamites invest these animals with a great emotional meaning. Their cattle are not used for meat, and a man's prestige depends on the size of his herds. Among the Mkamba the cattle are not slaughtered even if people are starving. In Uganda, just as in the *Odyssey*, the god owns herds of cattle.

The economic value of cattle in these culture areas is of

---

* Like phenomena from different cultures may have different meanings in their particular social contexts. It is believed, however, that in these instances there is considerable similarity of function.

secondary significance. Among the southern tribes cattle are used only as sacrificial offerings to the ancestral spirits, and the intense affection felt toward the animals amounts sometimes to a ritual veneration of the herds. Similar practices are related of the Xosa Kaffirs of South Africa, where the bull symbolizes the chief's power, and where every tribe has an ox from which it takes its name.

The Banyankole become warmly attached to their cows,[11] and in some instances these animals are petted, coaxed and loved like children; the death of a favorite cow causes grief and in some instances melancholia. Frankfort asserts that the cow represents a mother image. Among the Nilotic tribes, such as the Nuer, and probably among the southern Bantu, cattle are treated in the same way as we treat pets. An ox toward which a person is particularly affectionate may be named after a friend or a lover, and decorated with ornaments. Among the southeastern Bantu an intimate bond exists between a group and its cattle; cattle are the most important media for all ritual relations between human groups. Among the Zulus and Pondo, the drinking of milk among individuals establishes a blood brotherhood.

The prosperity of the entire tribe is bound up with the herd, which is protected by magical practices. In the Ngoni Highlands of South Africa, cattle primarily represent security in social, economic, and legal status, and are vitally needed in the rituals of the ancestor worship.[12] A practice sometimes found in the East African culture is the wrapping of the dead king in the skin of sacrificial cattle. Otto Rank has interpreted such customs as a symbolic return to the maternal womb.[13] It would seem likely that the cattle are identified with the deceased parents, for the dead body is associated with a beast whose flesh is eaten by the mourners.

Other striking similarities between certain African cultures and early Greece and Rome are the existence of comparable practices connected with the sacred fire, the religious functions of the king, and the magical making of rain by the priests. Rites of blood brotherhood are carried out by drinking a mixture of

blood and milk from cattle, and social position is to a great
extent based on ownership of cattle. These animals are used for
tribute, payment of taxes, and for legal compensations, and are
eaten only in religious rites.[14] Complete parallels to these latter
legal and sociological functions of cattle existed, as we shall see,
in Graeco-Roman antiquity.

The southeastern Bantu society[15] is particularly illustrative
of many of these similarities. The deepest values of the culture
are expressed in the tradition established by the dead ancestors,
and these values are periodically revivified in sacrificial rites
with cattle, which bind each individual emotionally to the community. The deified ancestors continue to enter into tribal matters
after their death; they are represented in the family worship
by the father, and in the national worship by the king-priest.
The chief is also a magician, and is regarded as the father of the
tribe. As the representative of the group's tradition, the king
possesses ancient sacred objects which serve as a type of regalia,
and he is often identified with an ox which is believed to embody
the dead ancestors. He is responsible for rainfall and the growth
of the crops. No conclusive proofs, however, have been found for
the ritual killing of the chief after he has held office for a given
period or after he has shown signs of weakness.* The king is
the owner of the sacred fire, which is a symbol of social unity
handed down by the earliest ancestor, the culture hero.

These culture traits—the veneration of cattle, the use of
cattle as sacrificial offerings in the ancestral cult, the sacred fire,
and the magician-king—are, as we have said, obviously very
reminiscent of the ancient Greek and Roman cultures, as is the
establishment of blood brotherhood through cattle rituals. But
what is of greatest interest is the role of cattle as a unit of value
and as a measure of social status, for it is at this point, in
classical antiquity, that we encounter the ritual symbols which
were the forerunners of coinage.

---

* Among the Shilluk, where the son could at any time challenge his
father to a combat for the kingship, the sacrificial bull represented the
first king, who was called father and worshiped as a god.

ten

THE RITUAL PREDECESSORS OF COINAGE

1. CATTLE AS A UNIT OF MONEY

The bull was a widespread unit of value in the early history of the Graeco-Roman culture.[1] Representations of ox heads in a palace inventory from Cnossus indicate that the ox unit was probably used in Crete in Minoan times. In Homer values are invariably expressed in terms of oxen. The arms of Diomedes are declared equivalent to nine oxen; those of Glaucos to 100. Female slaves skilled in crafts sold for four oxen, and the three-legged pot was worth twelve. A shipload of Lemnian wine was sold for cattle and hides. The laws of Draco in Athens stated fines in terms of cattle. In early Italy all objects were valued, accounted for, and paid for in cattle and sheep. It was only at about 452 B.C. that the law provided that fines and taxes stated in cattle and sheep could be paid for in pieces of marked copper.[2]

Many of our modern terms pertaining to monetary matters are derived from the use of cattle as a unit of value in ancient times. For example, the Latin *pecunia* is derived from *pecus* (cattle), as is the word "peculation." The term "fee" is believed to be ultimately derived from the Gothic *faihi,* denoting cattle. Likewise, the Indian *rupee* stems from a Sanskrit word meaning cattle. The economists' term "capital" and the legal word "chattel" stem from *capitale,* which originally designated cattle counted by the head. Similar etymologies have been suggested for the Teutonic and Scandinavian languages.

2. THE ABSENCE OF
AN EARLY MARKET SYSTEM

It has been well known to scholars for many years that in ancient times the bull functioned both as a unit of value and as a representative of the god. Why did this animal play two such apparently disparate parts at the same time? The answer given by Professor Bernhard Laum, an eminent German philologist, whose theories we shall shortly consider, is that the bull's significance as a unit of value arose from the religious rituals in which the flesh of a sacrificial bull was shared by the communicants according to ancient standards of justice.

The fact that these two seemingly unrelated functions of the bull, economic and religious, were never meaningfully linked together until Laum possibly reflects a deep spiritual trend in our culture which has resulted in a complete divorce, both in theory and in practice, between economic and religious life. The conception of the sacredness of human relations, economic, social, and political, has almost completely disappeared from our thought; as we explained in an earlier chapter, the Holy Grail appears to have vanished from the land.

Ancient economic life was imbedded within the larger framework of the goals of civilization, and was not dissociated from the ideals of the culture. Price in the modern sense did not exist, for exchange ratios were not the result of a self-regulating market mechanism kept in motion by a supposedly unlimited and universal desire for profit, but were believed to stem from the love (*philia*) and justice necessary for the maintenance and promotion of the community.

Many economic historians have not envisaged a complex organization of economic activity based on any institutional foundation other than the highly developed market system such as exists today. Recent studies, however, indicate that commerce as we now know it was very likely an invention of the Greeks. Prior to this innovation, economic transactions were carried out along the lines of patriarchal redistribution, traditionally determined equivalences of interchange (as in kinship reciprocities), and through long-distance movements of goods based on values fixed by custom or state authority. The "trader," in the sense of a bargainer for profit, did not exist in early times.*

3. RELIGIOUS IMAGERY ON EARLY COINS

The religious basis for the images on ancient Greek and Roman coins has long been accepted by most numismatists,[4] many of whom, however, seem to assume the existence of a full-

---

* This material is drawn from *Trade and Market in the Early Empires*,[3] which is strongly recommended to the reader for an extensive consideration of these ideas. Karl Polanyi's essay "Aristotle Discovers the Economy" (pp. 64-94) shows that economic practices were at first believed to be based on notions of love and justice.

fledged market system in antiquity, in which coinage was therefore introduced as a device to facilitate trade. The orthodox
point of view of these historians of money is that the type on
the coin was the state's guarantee that a certified weight and
quality of precious metal was present.[5] The symbols of the god
on the coin were an invocation of the deity to vouch for the
trustworthiness of the minting authorities. The minting of coins
was hence preceded by a traffic in bars of bullion, which were
weighed by those who engaged in barter. Some form of trade
in metals existed in Egypt, Babylonia, and Assyria.

The first coins were produced from an abundant natural alloy
of gold and silver called *electrum,* and most numismatists accept
Herodotus' statement that the Lydians in Asia Minor were the
first to engage in minting. Theorists differ as to whether the
issuing agents were originally private individuals such as bankers
or merchants,[6] or the state authorities. In the instance of Lydia,
whatever may have been the case beforehand, coinage was by
the time of Croesus in the hands of the king. By the middle of
the seventh century B.C., Aegina, an important commercial
center, had begun to mint coins, and before long many cities had
their own mints. The middle of the fifth century found the
issuing of coinage a common practice throughout the Greek
world. It should be mentioned here that coinage arose inde-
pendently in two regions other than Asia Minor and Greece: in
China, at about 1091 B.C.; and in India in the fourth century
B.C. A consideration of these other origins of coinage, however,
is outside of the scope of this book, as are the numerous forms
of money found among primitives all over the globe.

Various suggestions have been offered by numismatists as to
the manner in which ancient coinage originated.

One theory is that the coin type was the badge of the issuing
state, impressed like a city seal or the seal of a city magistrate
upon a lump of precious metal.[7] The custom of using signets to
be affixed as seals on property goes back to the earliest times,
and was certainly employed to symbolize the establishment of
sacred covenants long before the origin of coinage. The My-

cenaeans were familiar with the signet as a property mark, as were the Athenians, and according to Herodotus the Babylonians of the fifth century carried a signet. There is little doubt that such practices were familiar to the Lydians.

Armorial bearings were used extensively by ancient individuals, tribes, and cities, and some early coin types were identical with the arms of the city at which they were minted.[8] It is quite possible that some of the magistrate's symbols which are found upon the coins of antiquity were the hereditary crests of the great families, no doubt because of the dominance of the aristocrats in the ancient cities. In such cases the town arms and the family crest had the same significance. The ancestral cult of the ancient city seems to have played an important part in coin types, for great events in the city's history and beloved features of the city were often depicted on its coinage.

Coinage was early associated with the goddess Astarte, who was related to the Babylonian Mylitta and to the Greek Aphrodite, Artemis, and Hera. Indeed, according to Curtius,[9] the origin of coinage is to be traced to the cult of the great mother goddess of Sardia. The lion of the coins of Croesus was a symbol of this maternal divinity, who was closely connected with many commercial enterprises in ancient times as a protecting deity and patroness.

It has often been suggested by numismatists that the religious symbolism on the ancient coins resulted from the invention of coinage by the priesthoods, who first engaged in minting to expedite their commercial transactions. The emblems on the coins would symbolize both the god who was worshiped in the temple where the money was issued, and the city coat-of-arms: heraldry and religion were one and the same.

The treasury of the temple originated to a large extent from consecrations and bequests, and the priests utilized these offerings in banking operations to increase the wealth of their institution. Famous shrines of antiquity, such as the temple of Athena at Athens, that of Apollo at Delphi, and the temple of Juno Moneta at Rome functioned as banks and treasuries; and the priests therefore had in their possession large quantities of the precious metals. Since many of these great shrines were the centers of large scale pilgrimages, these temples became also the site of trade and commerce, which necessitated the impressing of a religious symbol upon pieces of gold and silver to facilitate the exchange of these objects in business transactions within the temples.

4. THE SACRIFICIAL MEAL AS FORERUNNER OF COINAGE

Apart from the tendency of many of the numismatists to project back into history our modern market system, the point of view that coinage originated in the temples is what we would naturally anticipate from our knowledge that the priest-king was the director of the economic life of the ancient city. We should certainly expect, in addition, the existence of some historical continuity between the common meal at the temple altar, which was the center of the giving and taking activities of the early community, and the minting of coinage by the priesthood.

The sacrifice to the god, according to Laum,[10] was a type of exchange with the deity, similar to the reciprocities among individuals. The ancient man made offerings to the deity, in return for which he expected to obtain such benefits as a good harvest and protection against sickness and other dangers. In the higher aspects of Greek religion the relation between man and god assumed a noble ethical character.

The offering of votive objects to the deity was not rigidly fixed in ancient Greece, but this was the case in early Rome, where the favors which could be received from the god were obtainable for a definitely prescribed sacrificial dedication. The god was here the master, and the votary brought him tribute as an offering. This relationship became transformed in the course of time into a regular exchange controlled and governed by the priests in accordance with the religious laws.

As in *Leviticus,* the animal victim which was brought to the god had to conform to painstakingly described rules; otherwise the ritual was of no avail. The offering was thus of a very definite type and character, a valuable good of rigidly determined quality. Insofar as atonement was the object of the votary, this good served as a fixed unit of absolution or propitiation: in a legal sense it functioned as a payment in an exchange between man and god.

The state religion, in establishing a carefully prescribed medium of exchange in the relationship between humans and the deity, thereby created a good of guaranteed economic worth, which could serve as a just, legal unit of value. The bull was the official sacrificial good in the Greek and Roman civilization, as well as in India. At first this animal offering functioned only in the relationship between the state and its god, but it is apparent that the existence of the bull unit of value would naturally lend itself to transactions on the periphery of the sacred commerce in the temple. Gradually, it is to be presumed, the norm of value created by the religious cult was carried over into secular exchanges, the bull becoming the standard unit of value in all obligations and debts among the inhabitants of the country. When metals were first introduced into the Graeco-Roman world, their value was reckoned in terms of the bull.

The share in the bull's flesh at the public meal also constituted a legal means of payment. The word *nomos,* which in later times signified the sacred law of the community, originally meant "distribution," and denoted the division of the sacrificial offering. Similarly, the term *dais,* which was applied to the holy meal, was also the word for "distribution." As we know, the god received part of the flesh of the sacrificial animal at the municipal sacred repast, the remainder of the bull being distributed among the participants in the ritual. The laws of the state cult stipulated precisely the manner of apportionment to the gods, to the presiding authorities, and to the citizens.

The priests as state officials were entitled to a reward for their services, and the citizens at large, as members of the state, had a legal right to participate in the division of the sacrificial flesh. The portion of the body of the victim functioned as an economic payment made legitimate through the justice of the state in the ritual distribution. The portion which each communicant received expressed his worth, the degree of his esteem in the group. That is to say, to the order of social rank there corresponded an order of rank in the apportionment of the roasted flesh, each person receiving a share commensurate with his status. The officials received the more honored parts of the sacrificial bull. The term *kolakretai,* designating the Athenian financial officials, originally meant "receivers of limbs."[11] Thus, one of the first forms of social organization in ancient times was the sacred *Nomos,* the division of the sacrificial animal, in which the various parts of the victim served as definite units of value.

The common meal was the first type of public finance. The king, who usually originated as the head of the dominant household in the association of clans constituting the ancient city, was the embodiment of the state, and presided over the sacrificial repast in the temple, killing the bull, carving its flesh, and distributing the portions of its roasted body. Participation in the public meal represented the recompense which an individual received for the services he had rendered to the state. The bulls which were used for sacrificial animals were the first form of taxes, and all city obligations were met at the ceremony at the king's table.[12] The portions of sacrificial flesh upon the spit were the state's payment for contributions made by citizens. Indeed, each member of the community had a legal claim upon a share in the bull's flesh—receiving a part of the roast was a symbol of citizenship.

5. THE EMERGENCE OF SYMBOLIC FORMS

The animal victim was roasted on a spit called *obelos,* which was a necessary accessory of the public meal. For this reason, the inventory of the temples very often included these cooking implements. The temple of Hera at Argos, for example, contained spits which had been dedicated by King Pheidon.* In the course of time, the sacrificial meat on a spit, Laum conjectures, became known as an "obelos." The well-known Greek coin called the *obolos* hence originated in the spitted portion of the flesh of the sacrificial bull.

The tripods and pots which are mentioned in the Homeric epics as prizes in the games attained their honorific value because they too were originally used for sacrificial purposes—as utensils for holding portions of the sacrificial flesh. The value of these tripods and pots was measured originally in bulls. As time went on, various votive objects brought to the gods entered into secular transactions, their worth fixed in terms of the bull unit of value within the religious cult.†

Excavations have disclosed vast numbers of imitations of animals around the ancient altars. These animal miniatures were offered in the place of an actual sacrificial victim, in the magical

---

* Quiggin[13] compares this practice with the offering of spits at sacrificial feasts in Lapland and with the dedication of spears used in cattle sacrifices at Shilluk and Dinka shrines.

† Paul Einzig[14] offers as ethnological parallels to Laum's theory, "the pig currency of the New Hebrides, a highly developed primitive monetary system that owes its existence entirely to the sacrificial use of certain types of pigs. There the standard animal suitable to be sacrificed is strictly defined; its value is determined by a well-established scale. This, together with the steady demand for pigs for sacrificial purposes, has led to the development of the use of the sacrificial pigs as a store of value, medium of exchange, standard of value, and especially standard of deferred payments. And while it would be irreverent to the memory of the Homeric heroes to bracket them with the savages of Oceania, the fact that the latter had worked out an elaborate monetary system on lines in accordance with Laum's theory could well be used in support of the theory that at a much earlier pre-Homeric stage of the Aegean civilization monetary evolution proceeded on similar lines. After all, during the period described by Homer the system appears to have been well established and it may have taken a thousand years to reach that stage. In this connection it is worth mentioning that in parts of French Indo-China the primitive currencies used until comparatively recently by backward races were cattle, tripods and cauldrons, which is identical with the system that operated in the Homeric age; this fact also indicates the possibility of the Homeric system originating through sacrificial requirements."

belief that the imitation would serve as a gift to the god as well as the real object. The purpose of these little figurines was hence to serve in the transactions between man and god as a means of payment and atonement. Tripods and pots were also dedicated in miniature form, as were bull heads. The imitation votive objects, Laum suggests, were manufactured by the temple establishment, and were obtained for use as offerings by the votaries, who exchanged other goods for them. In the deepest layers at Olympia there are little pots in so huge a quantity that they are, next to the animal figurines, the most frequently found sacrificial gift.

Like the spits, the imitation offerings became units of value because of their connection with the sacred meal. It seems likely that the ancient Roman currency called the *as* acquired its name from a term meaning "a piece of roast." The double axe, regarded by some investigators as a form of money, is similarly to be explained. The axe and double axe are mentioned in the Homeric poems as prizes given to the heroes, but it is obvious from their construction that they were not used as weapons or tools. On the other hand, throughout Cretan and Mycenaean sacred art the double axe appears as a holy object, often in close connection with the head of a bull; so that it very possibly acquired its significance as a medium of exchange because it was used in killing the sacrificial bull. If this is true, the double axe is to be interpreted in the same fashion as the spit. It is known that double axes were dedicated as votive gifts by Periklytos at Delphi just as spits were offered by King Pheidon of Argos.

Finally, the iron money of the Spartans also stemmed from religious cult, originating in the sickle which was used in this city to kill the holy animal.[15] This sickle is encountered in Cretan-Mycenaean art as the sacrificial knife. As in the instances already cited, the sickle, because of its use in the bull sacrifice, became an early form of money.

Just as in the case of the double axe on Cyprus and Tenedos, the obolos at Argos and Athens, and the tripods and kettles at

Delphi and on Crete, so on Delos and in Sparta the sickle, because it was a sacred implement, became a form of money. The sickle money was holy money.

Thus there entered into exchanges between members of the community symbolic forms, whose original significance in religious rite was, with the passage of time, completely forgotten. These miniature substitutes for the sacrificial animal or for the ritual implements of the sacred meal were therefore the predecessors, and possibly the original forms of coined money. This would explain why the holy animal, in particular the bull or the bull's head, so often appeared on the early coins. According to Laum, the bronze fish money of Olbia[16] grew out of the previously existing ritual of offering fish as sacrificial gifts.* The frequent appearances of various animal figures on the types of ancient coins therefore stemmed from the fact that these animals were the original sacrificial offerings made at the temple of the god.

----

* It might be added that in many of the pagan religions of antiquity fish were regarded as sacred. In the Adonis cult they were used as funeral offerings, for example, and in Syria and Mesopotamia they symbolized luck and vitality. The priests of Atargatis in Syro-Phrygia ate them as holy food. For many centuries the priests of Oannes in Babylonia dressed themselves up as fish. In some instances, fish were the sacrificial food at the common meal, and represented the deity.[17]

eleven

COINS AS
RELIGIOUS MEDALS

1. THE MAGICAL SIGNIFICANCE OF GOLD

Gold has been a medium of exchange for thousands of years. Most economists explain this by the theory that, to be used effectively as a money, a material must be portable, durable, homogeneous, divisible, and easily distinguishable from spurious objects. It is apparent that the bull was not chosen as a monetary unit on these grounds.[1] Similarly, the precious metals, although they possess these qualities, were not originally employed as money as the result of these practical considerations. Instead, their value in economic transactions stemmed from the type of belief that we have previously referred to as the "fetishism of gold."

Ancient man possessed no knowledge of metallurgy, geology, or physical chemistry, but attributed a general magical potency to all stones, certain types containing special talismanic or miraculous properties because of their size, shape, color, or unique characteristics. The employment of precious stones in antiquity for the decoration of images of the deities and in religious ceremonies, particularly funeral rites, stemmed from the belief in their wondrous mystical virtues.[2] The use of stones as amulets was common among the ancient Greeks and Romans, and the employment of precious stones as ornaments stemmed from this magical practice.[3] In early Italy, for example, bronze adornments were believed to be capable of warding off evil spirits, and similar prophylactic uses of silver and gold existed.[4]

In the cultures of antiquity gold seems to have been first employed for ornamental purposes, its original value, according to G. Elliot Smith,[5] stemming from the magical qualities attributed to it by the ancient Egyptians. Gold was used very extensively for personal adornment in ancient Egypt and Babylonia.[6] Among the Jews gold was employed mainly for decorative, rather than for monetary purposes, and the gold imported by the Phoenicians was used largely for making ornaments, bracelets, in particular.[7] To this day, one of the main uses of the precious metals is in the earrings, bracelets, and finger rings worn by women to add to their "charm."

In ancient times, each of the metals existed in a mystic sympathy with an astral body, which exerted an influence upon its properties.[8] Gold had an astrological affinity with the sun, silver with the moon, iron with Mars, quicksilver with Mercury, tin with Jupiter, copper with Venus, and lead with Saturn. It was in Babylonia that these beliefs became particularly important. The theory has been advanced that the relation of the value of silver to gold in antiquity (1:13 1/3) was based on the relation of the course of the moon to the movement of the sun (27:360). The existence of such beliefs in ancient Greece is attested by remarks made both by Pindar and Proclus.

The sun and moon were regarded as deities in early Greek

popular belief;[9] indeed, one of the accusations made against Socrates was that he denied the divinity of these heavenly bodies. Both Pythagoras and Aristotle, on the other hand, accepted the belief in the divine nature of these celestial personalities, while Anaxagoras shocked the people by maintaining that the stars were merely incandescent bodies. Roman annals of great antiquity recorded the dedication of altars to the sun and moon by an early king, and a priest and priestess of the sun existed in Athens. As in Egypt, the Sun God in Crete took the form of a bull, and the Moon Goddess took the shape of a cow.[10]

The sun was often regarded as a royal body, particularly in Rome and Egypt, where the king was in certain periods worshiped as a Sun God. It seems reasonable to suppose that it was for this reason that gold became the symbol of illustrious regality in ancient times. In Egypt, for example, the king, as a representative of the god, "possessed the untarnished brightness of gold." The splendor of divine life was symbolized by gold, and this metal was identified with the sun, whose divinity was manifested on earth by the ruler.[11]

In any event, gold has been associated with the kingship since the earliest times. Both gold and silver have been regarded as the "noble," as distinguished from the "base" metals. In Plato's *Republic,* the individuals destined for the rulership of the ideal state are those in whose nature gold is present, the next most honorable people are of the silver type, and the less glorious persons are those composed of the base metals. A close relationship between gold and the majesty of the king is known to have existed in ancient Greece.[12] In general, any golden object magically radiated or diffused outward the vital *mana* of the royalty.*

---

* Hocart suggested[13] that gold was originally regarded as sacred because of its solar affinity, and that the circular form of the coin was the result of the fact that it magically represented the sun's disk. Coins were therefore originally amulets which were valued because of their mystic potencies. The heads of rulers appeared on the ancient coins because they were the representatives of the deity.

It is thus apparent that possession of a golden coin in ancient times played the same role as sharing in the sacrificial meal, making it possible for the communicant to identify with the king's divine powers, and, in Veblen's famous phrase, enabling the participant to "emulate his pecuniary betters."

2. THE ORIGINAL SIGNIFICANCE OF COINAGE

The word "money" stems from "Moneta," a name of the goddess Juno, in whose temple Roman money was minted. According to Laum, whose theories[14] we now resume, the stamped pieces of metal were called *monetae.* "Moneta" was also a name of the goddess Aequitas, who represented the *equity* or fair apportionment which the state granted to its citizens. Aequitas was thus a divinity governing the social organization expressed in the legal division of rights and duties in accordance with justice.

This derivation indicates that coinage originated in the distribution of rights and duties among the members of the community, first manifested in the sacrifice of the holy bull and the sharing of its flesh among the participants. In ancient times, the political unit was identical with the cult congregation: sharing in the sacrificial flesh was the most sacred right and most important privilege of the citizen-communicant. In early Greece and Rome, as we have seen, the portion of the holy victim constituted a type of fee, reward, or gift which the state (the temple) distributed to citizens and officials.* Exclusion from the common meal was a disgrace.

The oldest altar to Moneta was located on Mons Albanus, where a bull sacrifice, the central ritual of the Latin confederacy, was annually held. The manner of division of the sacrificial victim was believed to be of the utmost importance—the ritual had to be repeated if the portions were not equally distributed among the participants. Since the first form of money consisted

---

* Similar attitudes existed in early China.

of the just apportionment of the sacrificial bull, the minting of Roman coinage in the temple of Moneta was the result of the perpetuation of the traditional idea of the fair distribution of goods among the members of the cult community.

The first coins were religious medals, serving not as media of circulation in commerce, but functioning in the same fashion as the portion of food distributed at the sacred meal.

Medals were given by the king to his subjects as a sign of esteem and honor, and symbolized the contribution made by an individual to the state. The fineness of quality of these medals stemmed from the ruler's desire to bestow upon his subjects a gift of the highest possible perfection. Status determined the metal of which a particular medal would consist: the greatest honor was to receive a gold medal, followed by bestowals of silver and bronze.

These early coins, or medals, also functioned as royal remembrances or souvenirs. Indeed, the words "monument" and *moneta* are closely connected etymologically. The king would give his portrait to loyal subjects as an expression of a close personal relationship. Like other ancient works of art, coins functioned as memorials, serving to immortalize an important, highly regarded person or occurrence. Thus the distribution of a medal bearing the portrayal of a king would serve both as a commemoration (monument) and as a mark of the ruler's affection for his people. The image upon the coin was hence not originally a sign guaranteeing the value of the metal, but was an expression of a dear friendship, a symbol of the emotional bond between giver and receiver.

Part of the religious significance of the early coins stemmed from the fact that the stamped metal carried the *mana* of the king.* The royal personage was filled with a magic potency which carried over into all of his doings, and every object he came in contact with overflowed with this power. The economic

---

* The British crown-pieces bearing the head of King Charles I were believed to possess healing powers equivalent to the royal touch for curing the "King's Evil."[15]

value of a particular object was irrelevant to its mystic properties, which remained in every part of that object even if its
economic value was destroyed.

Coins, therefore, originally served as charms possessing
magical powers. The use of coins as amulets is very well known,
the possessor of the coin believing himself charmed against
sickness, poverty, and danger. In the Middle Ages this belief was
highly prevalent. Holy coins were often distributed at the church
festivals in the Middle Ages. Coins to protect the holder from
plagues were also given out by the church, and similar practices
existed in ancient Rome. For example, about 190 A.D. coins were
distributed, bearing the picture of Apollo, the god of healing.
The coins bestowed as gifts on many holy occasions by the king
and the royal family possessed a magical value too because of
the sacred nature of the givers.

Another contributing factor in the evolution of coinage was
the signet ring. As has been stated, the ring has been regarded,
from the earliest times to the present, as a magical device for
binding people together into a sentimental union. Friendship
between comrades was often expressed in this manner.

A typical gift of a king to his subject, the ring was highly
valued as a symbol of friendship in Egypt and Babylon, as well
as in northern Europe. The earliest form of the seal ring was
the scarab, which had an oval form like the early coins. Signet
rings were of great importance in the Cretan-Mycenaean culture,
and, in the course of the centuries, exerted a formative influence
upon the origin of coins, the signet eventually becoming the
image on the coin. The close mental association between rings and
money also existed in the Middle Ages, when the ring was a
cherished money token.

Money, states Laum, was thus originally a symbol which
created a deep sentimental union among individuals.* The
picture of the king upon the coin established a feeling of fidelity,
trust, and confidence between himself and his subjects, and

---

* The term for this symbolism, *gemeinschaftbildend,* which appears in
Laum's text, is particularly apt.

brought together all members of the community in an identification with a common ideal image. Like the ring, the coin was a symbol which bound the citizens to one another in warm emotional ties. Similar feelings existed in the Middle Ages toward the patron saints who appeared on the coins of the political units.

Since the ancient city was a union based on the worship of a common god, the distribution of coins bearing the image of the community's protective divinity brought each individual into communion with the deity. The portion of the sacrificial animal in early times established this union with the god, and the coin in later periods was simply a continuation of this communion between man and the divine powers.* Indeed, the share in the

---

* Salt in antiquity possessed a religious symbolism closely analogous to that of the early coin medals. Public officials and soldiers in ancient Rome were often paid in the form of salt, and it seems likely that the term "salary" and such phrases as "to be worth one's salt" are derived from the Roman word "salarium."

In early days, salt was believed to possess magical qualities, and for this reason played an important part in religious rituals and covenants.[16] Homer speaks of salt as a divine substance, and Plato describes it as being especially dear to the gods. Primitives often regard salt as a symbol of the procreative element in the male sexual fluid, and numerous allusions of this type are to be found in folklore.[17]

Salt was an essential constituent of sacrificial offerings in ancient Egypt, Greece, and Rome. The Greeks and Latins sprinkled salt on the head of the sacrificial animal. Salt was mixed with the sacrificial cakes, and was dissolved in water for lustrations. In fact, in Greece, salt was given to the gods as a thanks-offering before every meal.[18]

The religious significance of salt as a necessary part of the sacrificial offering and as a means of establishing covenants is clearly indicated in several passages in the Old Testament. For the Arabs, the mutual partaking of salt created a holy bond, and was one of the most sacred acts in which a person could engage. In ancient Greece also, salt was used to confirm oaths and compacts, and in various parts of the world, as well as in antiquity, this material has served as a symbol of friendship.

The evil consequences of spilling salt at the table were a belief of the ancient Greeks and Romans. In Rome there was a religious prohibition against setting any food upon the table until the salt had been placed; and, because of the magical properties of salt and its use as a sacrificial offering, the salt cellar was regarded as a holy vessel. Even the status of guests was indicated by their distance from the salt on the table. Thus, salt, like

holy flesh and afterward the distribution of the coin impressed with the image of the deity brought about and reaffirmed the mutual identification with the creative powers of nature which was the very basis for the existence of the ancient community.

3. THE CIRCULATION OF CULT SYMBOLS

The institution of coinage arose out of the public distribution of the flesh of the sacrificial animal. But exactly how did this evolution take place? Very little is known about the detailed answer to this question, which involves such problems as the origin of the market* and the role which was played by the "metics" (foreign settlers) in the economic life of the ancient city.

We do know, on the authority of Herodotus,[20] that the beginnings of coinage and the first retailing of food were closely connected. It is also known that generals would often provision their armies during campaigns by encouraging agents to set up markets to dispense food to the soldiers in return for some form of money presumably provided by their officers. Charity to the poor was carried out by public distributions of food. From these origins, it may have been that in the populous centers, as in the agora at Athens, there gradually came into being a class of individuals who made it a practice of offering food in return for some unit of value originally distributed among the populace by the authorities. It is in these symbols given to the members of the community as a reward or as a right of citizenship, legally permitting them to obtain food at the common meals, that we might look for the origin of coinage.

A number of instances are known in which practices of this

---

the early coins, served in antiquity as a sign of honor, as a religious symbol, as a mark of *gemeinschaft*, and as a unit of value.

(The use of salt as a money, a frequently encountered practice among primitives, is beyond the scope of our considerations here.)

* Chapter Fourteen contains a discussion of the origin of the market. The reader is again referred to *Trade and Market in the Early Empires.*[19]

type were probably carried out, as for example the method whereby the treasurers of the city goddess compensated the judges for their services at legal proceedings. In addition to receiving the staff of office upon entering the court of justice, each citizen received a *symbolon* (token), which he gave up to the prytane after the proceedings were ended, obtaining his money in return.[21] Laum suggests that this custom stemmed from the earlier payment of officials in the form of a portion of sacrificial flesh.* Originally, upon entering the proceedings, each participant would receive an iron spit, or *obelos*, which would signify that he was entitled to a share in the sacrificial animal; when he finished the sitting, the citizen would receive a portion of flesh from the prytane.[23]

Another practice which indicates how the transition from sacrificial flesh to money may have occurred is to be found in the custom of the royal and aristocratic Roman families of distributing gifts in the form of *monetae* on festive occasions.[24] This gift was called a *sportula*, which literally means "basket." The reason for this derivation is that these distributions from the prominent families originally took the form of a common meal, at which food was distributed in baskets. The status of the participant in the distribution determined the type of sportula which he received. In some instances, which perhaps were intermediate points in the transition between sacrificial flesh and coinage, both a portion of food and a sportula were distributed. The fact that the private treasury of the emperor was called *fiscus* (from which our modern "fiscal" is derived) is significant, for the term *fiscus* also stems from the word for "basket." In the course of time, it is to be presumed that the distribution of food by the ruler was transformed into the distribution of coins.

---

* Despite the introduction of money, the natural economy persisted up to at least 412 B.C. Town wages were for a long time paid in food. Throughout Greece the priests received as payment a part of the tithe and a share in the sacrificial animal.[22]

4. CULT TOKENS AS "MEAL TICKETS"

Additional evidence, drawn from customs in different periods and places, may also be drawn upon to support, through analogy, Laum's general point of view and to suggest the manner by which coinage may have evolved from sacrificial communion rites.

We have seen that the ancient city and its constituent units, the *gens*, or clans, were religious groups, and the devotion of the individual to his community and to its tradition was expressed in cult symbolism. Membership in the religious life of the community, at first directly expressed in participation in food rituals, was later represented by symbolic forms: coinage was an outgrowth of these religious symbols.

Tokens signifying that the bearer was a member of a religious brotherhood were common among the people of antiquity.[25] For example, in the Gnostic sect founded by Basilides about 110 A.D., tokens engraved with the name "Abraxas," a word with mystical significance, were given to neophytes as a symbol of their membership in the cult, and were believed to endow the initiates with miraculous powers. Tokens were used, according to Shiells, to identify the individuals who had been initiated into the Eleusinian Mysteries, as well as other ancient cults.

These ancient tokens were made of various materials, frequently of metal. The Roman "tesserae" were given to the victors in the public games as a sign that they were entitled to be supported by the state for the remainder of their lives. Tesserae were also given to the poor as a certificate that they were permitted to receive a portion in the public allotment of grain. At the time of Augustus, tesserae in the form of coins were distributed, entitling an individual either to a quantity of corn or to a sum of money; it was possible for a person to give his tesserae to another, thereby legally enabling the receiver to obtain a portion of corn at the public distribution.[26] From later sources it is probable that these tesserae, whether they served in the distribution of corn or of money, had the same appearance as money and were shaped like money.[27] Money-shaped tesserae appeared in bronze and lead, and had as a type-face the head of Caesar or members of his family.

Tesserae were used in Rome for admission to the games, following the time of Augustus; and in Greece the *symbola* (equivalent to the Roman tesserae) were employed as a token of admittance to the theater. In Athens they served to enable a person to enter the theater of Dionysus. The Athenian *symbola* were also used for entrance to the public meetings.

In Rome tesserae were employed by the corporations (religious industrial organizations analogous to the medieval guilds) for admission to the sacred meals and rituals. The large Roman households also distributed tesserae to their clients, who could exchange them externally for real money.

Other types of tesserae were used as gifts on New Year's, and bore phrases of felicitation for the festival. The *tesserae nummariae* served a function similar to our modern bills of exchange, and the *tesserae conviviales* were similar to cards of invitation to a banquet, being presented at the door of the house of the host.

Among the most interesting of these symbolic forms were the *tesserae hospitales,* which were a sign of the existence of intimate bonds of loyalty between two families. Such a *tessera* gave the holder a claim on the protection of the allied household, and was inherited as an heirloom. Tesserae were also used in Byzantine churches, convents, and other religious institutions.[28]

The image of the goddess Fortuna often appeared on the privately issued tesserae in the act of distributing material goods, and it is known that this divinity was closely associated with Moneta. It is apparent that the tesserae were actually cult tokens,[29] symbols expressing membership in a religious communion. For every institution in ancient times, whether it was the family, state, corporation, theater, the public games, an intra-family agreement, or a client-patron relation, was a religious association or communion, membership in which was symbolized by receiving a share of food in the common meal.

5. TOKENS IN THE CHRISTIAN CHURCHES

We might mention in conclusion two analogous practices[30] which, though drawn from later times, are also highly suggestive of the evolution of symbolic forms from the ancient sacrificial meal.

The *méreau* or *jeton de présence,* was a token given to the Roman Catholic clergy as a record of their participation in the mass, in the canonical hours, and in other official duties, in order that they might receive payment for their services. These symbols were usually made of lead, copper, or brass, and carried inscriptions and types of a religious nature. Other types of tokens were distributed by numerous religious groups as symbols entitling the holder to certain funds or privileges. The use of *méreaux* is mentioned in France in 1375, and probably extended much further back in time; they were widely used in France and the Low Countries for many centuries in abbeys, convents, hospitals, infirmaries, parish churches, and confraternities.

Méreaux were turned in for cash at various intervals, and in some instances could be exchanged for food. They often had a small circulation within the religious body. In a number of cases it was customary for religious officials to give *méreaux* as alms, enabling the poor to exchange these tokens for victuals. This produced a tendency for the circulation of *méreaux* to be extended outside of the religious body into the town itself. It is a matter of dispute whether, in some places in the Low Countries, certain pieces in regular circulation were church *méreaux* or base coins.

Méreaux have at times been used in the Roman Catholic Church as tokens admitting the holder to the communion. This usage, however, has been much more prevalent in the Protestant Church, where they have been used extensively as certifications admitting the worthy members of the congregation to communion. In the Walloon Church at Amsterdam, these tokens (called *tesserae* in the first Helvetic confession) were used as signs that a person had satisfactorily been examined as to his religious knowledge and moral character, and was therefore to be admitted to the communion. The inscriptions were of a religious nature, showing such images as a chalice or a shepherd feeding his flock.

Méreaux employed as communion tokens were widely used in France, particularly from 1740 to 1840. In England, communion tokens were employed as early as 1559. The use of these symbolic forms was also extensive in later times in Ireland and in the United States.[31] In the Church of Scotland, for example, no one was allowed to be present at holy communion unless he had a communion token, which was given out by the elders after examinations testing the person's good character and knowledge of the religious precepts. Persons under disqualification were not given tokens, and hence could not attend communion. Churches in large towns displayed the city arms along with the religious symbols on these consecrated medals. Communion tokens in Scotland performed a function similar to the ancient *tesserae hospitales,* in that a person leaving a parish would carry its tokens with him as an introduction to his new parish.

In fifteenth century England communion tokens circulated indiscriminately with tradesmen's tokens, which were issued by tradesmen to be used as small change. In some instances, the church dues were collected by selling communion tokens, as for example in Southwark, where, in 1596, 2200 tokens were sold for two pence each.

6. COINS AS RELIGIOUS TOKENS

In all of these later practices—*méreaux,* communion tokens, and tesserae—we see examples of coin-shaped symbolic forms which not only expressed membership in a religious communion ritual but which were closely associated with the economic institutions of the time. Of course, we can mention these customs only to provide interesting analogies, and we must wait for further research to reveal to us in detail the course of the social evolution which led from the sacrificial meal to the medal which later entered into circulation to become currency.

But the fact of this evolution seems to us to be well established, even though we cannot account for all of the steps in this transition. It should be kept in mind that in ancient times, because of the belief in sympathetic magic, there was no distinction made between a symbol and that which the symbol represented. Hence, possession of a cult symbol was identical, magically speaking, to actual participation in the ritual; and therefore the medal, or certificate of membership, was emotionally equivalent to the share in the sacrificial flesh.

By entering into general circulation, these tokens of admittance to the ritual distribution of food began to break down the narrow circle of mutual aid among kinship groups and local political units. It now became possible for these symbols to pass into the hands of all people, and hence, increasingly through the centuries, all men began to be drawn into a world-wide sharing of production and consumption. So that money, although it has largely become a symbol of universal "otherhood" rather than brotherhood,[32] did indeed originate in the same manner as the Holy Grail, as the ideal of a universal holy communion.

PART **5**

Money in the Holy Community

twelve

MONEY AND GRACE

1. THE IDEALS IN MONEY

The everyday five-dollar bill, crumpled, worn, and worthless in itself, possesses its value not simply because it was printed by the Treasury Department, but because it is backed by the resources of the United States. And perhaps the soundest of these resources is the inherited religious capital symbolized on our money.

If we pause for a moment in the midst of our commercial transactions, we can notice upon one side of the five-dollar bill a picture of Abraham Lincoln, partially framed in two sprays of wheat, and on the other side a depiction of the Lincoln Memorial in Washington, D.C. This magnificent structure, standing on a terraced mound in Potomac Park opposite to the Washington Monument, is in the architectural style of an ancient

Greek temple. Surrounding the building are thirty-six Doric columns, surmounted by state seals, representing the states in the union at the time of Lincoln's death, and on the walls above the colonnade, supported at intervals by eagles, are memorial festoons. On the pedestals alongside the steps in front of the memorial are tripods holding a bowl, and dimly under the great pillars we can make out Lincoln himself, seated in majestic repose. In back of the President, not discernible on the picture, is the legend:

IN THIS TEMPLE
AS IN THE HEARTS OF THE PEOPLE
FOR WHOM HE SAVED THE UNION
THE MEMORY OF ABRAHAM LINCOLN
IS ENSHRINED FOREVER

Underneath Lincoln's hands, which rest firmly upon the arms of the chair, are two bundles of rods bound together. These ancient Roman symbols of political unity are also found on the penny, which bears imagery akin to the five-dollar bill, in the form of the mottoes, "In God We Trust" and "E Pluribus Unum."

We have previously likened the sprays of wheat surrounding the portrayal of Lincoln to the attributes of the ancient god of vegetation whose powers insured the prosperity of the land. Similarly, the tripod and bowl devices, called "paterae" by the Romans, are images in a tradition thousands of years old. These utensils were used in antiquity to hold the sacrifices which were offered to the god who lived within the temple, and which were shared among the participants in the public meal. The paterae, it is evident, were a type of grail, a holy vessel containing a magical, life-giving food.

These motifs on our modern money are not just decorations, but are symbols of ideas and sentiments of profound significance in economic history.

In antiquity the word *entheos* was used to describe a participant in the sacrificial communion feasts in which a god in animal form was killed and eaten, and the verb form of this term was *enthousiazein,* meaning "to become engodded"[1]—"to become one with the god." This is the origin of our modern word "enthusiasm." Identification with the divine powers symbolized in the sacred meal was the source of the energy and strength of character of ancient man.

Commitment to the tradition of cultural advancement enables an individual to achieve his maximum self-actualization, for it is only by devoting himself to a higher cause that he can integrate his personality and attain complete emotional fulfillment.[2] The work of Durkheim[3] indicates that the meaning of life is to be found in being part of a community, without which existence loses its vitality and richness. The shared enthusiasm and the mutual appreciation within a healthy group give each individual a feeling of warmth, love, and emotional security, whereas nonbelonging tends to make life seem lonely, futile, and empty. The good community inspires its members to feel affection and respect for other people, and causes each person to devote his energies to helping others, not out of a sense of obligation, but out of the spontaneous inner abundance which is the only firm basis for all of law and ethics.*

The source of human value is thus the creative energies of the cosmos, which tend to bring about increasing levels of order in the universe, and hence constitute a natural law immanent in all of being. The belief in a divine order is expressed in the emotional commitment of each individual to the welfare of the community, and hence underlies all forms of justice, social organization, and law. In the institutions centering around the sharing of food, early man received many of his first intimations of a power of rational love controlling his instincts, and to this

---

* The ideal community which is here envisaged does not in any way obliterate the individual. We construe a community as "good" only if it promotes individual freedom of conscience and self-actualization. When a community fails to express this ethical value, it is no longer a "good" community, and it is each person's right and duty to withdraw from or to rebel against this group.

degree the early forms of money which evolved from the ritual meal symbolized the divine cosmic order.

Natural law, as we conceive it, provides the invariant principle of human relations from which stem the specific laws of human societies. These specific laws, developed by each community, must be changed from time to time to fulfill their essential purpose of promoting the vitality of the group.

For the maintenance of justice within the community, each person must behave in a rational manner, that is, every individual must identify himself as part of a divine order, thereby devoting his instinctual energies to the enhancement of the common welfare. This requires that every individual possess the courage to assert his rights, the strength of character to step aside when another individual is better qualified for a certain honor, and the intelligence necessary to evaluate the needs and merits of other people.

In this context, "reason" is a person's ability to control his impulses in accordance with the laws necessary to maintain the institutions within which all individuals can attain their maximum self-actualization. The organization of the obtaining and distributing of food in early times was symbolic of the divine order in nature, for it required the mastery of the appetites by a conception of the order needed to maintain justice in the community.*

Early man's first idea of natural law resulted from the projection of his social organization into the cosmos. Cornford,[4] following Durkheim, has shown that in early Greece the conception of nature was derived from notions of human destiny within the community. The very word *cosmos*, in fact, was originally a political term. Thus, religion and law were originally one, both arising from the ancestral tradition.

The rational aspect to the projection of the social organiza-

---

* The word "rational" is related to the term "ration," which signifies a portion of distributed food, and the concept of the *ratio*, from which is derived "ratiocination" (rational thought), may have developed from the apportionment of food by weighing.[5]

tion of the group into nature lay in the fact that it represented the germinal recognition of a universal natural law.[6] In his maturity, after centuries of abstraction, man would become aware, in scientific thought, of the creative forces in nature which cause the formation of progressively higher patterns of order in the universe. In the course of the development of ancient Greece and Rome, men gradually realized the irrationality of regarding their own local customs as divinely ordained, and ultimately, in Stoicism, came to recognize as inherent in the cosmos a universal reason shared by all men. Thus Stoicism paved the way for a universal brotherhood of man, based on the mutual identification of all men with the divine *logos*, which acted as a moral force governing every individual. This universal reason was symbolized by the divine fire, which was the extension of the symbol of political unity to include all nations.

2. JUSTICE AND THE VITALITY OF THE COMMUNITY

In the highest sense in which we can conceive it, early money was a symbol of justice—a symbol of the laws and social institutions which enable each individual to actualize his potentialities to the fullest possible extent commensurate with the self-realization of the other members of the group. Where justice prevails, there is a rationally changing order of work roles and statuses, and there is no frustration resulting from the refusal of other individuals to grant a particular person the advancement which he deserves. In such an ideal community, each participant is willing to make way emotionally if another individual merits a position of more importance than his own.

Justice enables each individual to feel secure that his efforts will be adequately appreciated, and to feel that he need not fear that others threaten his deserved advancement. The presence of security and the absence of fear cause every man to possess a feeling of vitality and spontaneous good will toward others. This is the state of grace.

Where justice does not exist in the apportionment of work tasks, however, the self-actualization of one or more members of the group is blocked. These individuals lose the feeling of oneness with the community, thereby losing the source of inspiration which gave vitality to their lives. Furthermore, the unjustly treated person comes to resent those who have benefited by the injustice done to him. Hostility arises, which further tends to disrupt the unity of the group. The result may be strife, or a mounting series of mutual injustices. Finally, every man tends to fear that the others threaten him; the feeling of warmth and vitality which each person originally obtained from the group disappears, and people are no longer motivated to devote their whole-hearted energies to the welfare of the community. There is a breakdown of the loving communion among the members of the group, and there results, to some degree, Hobbes' "war of every man against every man." Life loses its richness; and the individual, no longer sharing a common enthusiasm for a tradition of progress, tends to feel lonely and futile. He begins to feel that the only meaning in life is the pursuit of less enduring and satisfying pleasures, for the group, far from being a source of inspiration to creative devotion, is a source of frustration and fear.

A major cause of injustice is the immaturity of those individuals who have failed to accept in a spirit of rational love the instinctual restrictions and efforts required for the just community. The sociological effect of this immaturity is *anomie,* or lawlessness, a social situation in which no individual is secure in his self-actualization. In such a state, there is an absence of mutual appreciation; and each man, instead of taking the pains to consider the merits and needs of others, seeks by fair means or foul to acquire more power.

This condition of *anomie* is to a great extent caused by what the ancient Greeks called the sin of *hubris,* or insolence, which ". . . has its root in want of reverence and want of self-knowledge . . . [and] is the expression of a self-centered will recognizing

no law but its own impulses . . . This insolence in the Greek
tragedy is the deepest source of moral evil . . ."[7]

The immature desire to be omnipotent is equivalent to an
inability to accept emotionally the genuine claims of others to
social honor. Hubris results in a continual lawless struggle
among men which interferes with the common welfare and the
happiness of the members of the group. In this state of *anomie*,
law results only from force and fear—instinctual renunciations
are imposed upon men rather than being accepted freely in a
spirit of devotion to the community.

The struggle for power among individuals seeking omnipotence results in a continual warfare between the ruled and the
rulers. The hubris of the leader may cause the hatred of his
subjects, or the insolence of the subordinates may produce an
irrational rebellion against authority. Either the ruler or the
ruled, or both, may be morally at fault. We have dwelled at
length upon the ideals of the ancients, but the reality must often
have been that of a ruthless tyranny using an ideology to promote its own selfish ends. The citizen of early Greece and Rome
was completely controlled both in body and mind, and complete
conformity, even in style of dress, was required from each
person by the state. Religion, wrote Fustel de Coulanges, revealed gods everywhere, deities which crushed man under the
feet of their ill will, and which left him no liberty in his actions
or thoughts. For many centuries judicial regulations were not
even written down, and only the members of the great aristocratic families were allowed to interpret the law.[8]

3. THE ROOTS OF HUBRIS

What can psychoanalysis contribute to an understanding of
the causes of this hubris which hinders the development of social
institutions to facilitate justice?

In the individual's psychological development his first conceptions of a divine order of nature and his first attitudes toward social authority are molded by his early relations to his parents. In fact, according to Freud, the basis for the existence of any group is the mutual identification of each child with its parents,* and the transference of these images to other kinfolk. Artificial groups are constituted by an identification with a common parent image or a common ideal. The archaic primary group, he wrote, "is a number of individuals who have substituted one and the same object for their ego ideal and have consequently identified themselves with one another in their ego."[9]

The basis for early group psychology was the oral identification with the common maternal and paternal image, and it was for this reason that eating the sacrificial animal was at the focal point of all of ancient social organization. Identification is the first form of the mutual role-taking which underlies all communication, and is hence at the root of herd phenomena. In later life, of course, this identification matures into an intelligent understanding of other people.

The primitive community represents the body of the parent: by being a member of the group, an individual is able to remain attached to the mother and father. As Suttie[11] suggests, the desire to be part of a community is motivated by the need to avoid the loss of the mother's love, for each person in the group acts as a parent to everyone else. The division of labor and consumption, from this standpoint, is based upon each individual behaving as a parent toward all the others.

Freud's group psychology explains many of the characteristics of the immature community, whose members have not yet freed themselves from the influence of the parental images. In the archaic group, the leader, with whom each individual identifies, exerts a hypnotic-like effect upon each individual. The lack

---

* Psychoanalysis now speaks of a "combined parent figure" in the transferences active in group psychology,[10] and we shall hence regard Freud's theory of community formation as applying to the mother as well as the father, even though Freud spoke mainly of the paternal image in this connection.

of rationality, the dwindling of the critical powers, the loss of intelligent self-control, and the easy suggestibility of the members of this community result from the carrying-over of infantile habits toward the leader, who represents the parent image. Justice cannot exist in such a group, for the participants lack the capacity to accept instinctual renunciations,* and are without the insight into themselves and others which is necessary for the mature resolution of interpersonal conflicts of interest.

Furthermore, the immature individual often fails to make a rational assessment of the precepts instilled in him by his parents. Where these precepts constitute genuine moral virtues, no harm to the community results from this unexamined identification with the parental personality. However, where the superego reflects the shortcomings, prejudices, or mistaken conceptions of the parents, unreflective acceptance may result in irrational, rigid behavior in relation to other individuals. The lack of intelligent self-control stemming from blind obedience to ancestral custom also contributes to moral, intellectual, and technological backwardness within a society. The aristocrat is particularly prone toward hubris, for his family pride and the pressure of the ancestral tradition often give him a sense of exaggerated importance, and make it difficult for him to accept the merits of those whom he considers beneath him.

Psychologically speaking, law originates in the ties between children and their mother. Each of the siblings identifies himself with the mother insofar as he desires to promote the loving bonds within the family. As a result of the formation of the image of the just parent, there gradually emerges the abstract figure of justice itself, personified by a mother's image. The conceptions of divine law and justice in ancient times were first embodied by the figure of the goddess. This was the case in both Greece and Rome. In early Greece the notion of Law and Right was symbolized by the goddess Themis, the mother.[12]

---

* The Oedipal motivations in early group psychology are discussed in the next chapter.

The father image also plays an important part in the formation of these ethical conceptions, as is attested by the gods of justice encountered in many of the cultures of antiquity.

Where, however, the parent shows favoritism toward one child, disharmonies result within the family which distort the proper development within the children of the conception of justice in community life. The spoiled child fails to learn to appreciate the needs and abilities of others, and the neglected child, wounded and hurt, may become chronically resentful of everyone else. Separation anxiety—the fear of losing the love of its parents—is evoked in the child when it feels that the father or mother does not love all members of the family equally, and this anxiety may give rise to diverse infantilisms which in later life may seriously interfere with the operation of justice. The giving and taking of economic goods among adults may not express rationality and love, but may be motivated by masochistic and sadistic tendencies stemming from childhood problems.

Certainly, a great deal of the competitiveness of our society stems from the carrying-over of irrational sibling rivalries into adult life, and the character-trait of vanity, which motivates so much economic activity, results largely from early insecurities, hatreds, and desires for revenge. Ancient coinage, far from being a symbol of a divine cosmic order of justice, may in actual practice have been, like many primitive moneys, a type of decoration, medal, or charm by means of which individuals sought to attain higher status through ostentatious display.[13]

4. MONEY AND MODERN MAN

We may confidently predict that in the future money will increasingly symbolize human relations within large organizations. The era of the small, independent businessman is drawing to a close, and new institutions are needed to maintain and promote personal welfare within the giant bureaucracies which will be man's future economic habitat.

What will be the fate of the individual within these large organizations? Will he have the opportunity to exercise his creative capacities to the fullest possible extent, to be properly rewarded for his contributions to the social welfare, and to maintain the integrity necessary for his mental and emotional health?

We have sought to show that in antiquity economic behavior was enmeshed within the life of the culture, and subordinated, in a utopian sense, to man's ideals of the good life. Economics was embedded in sociology, and sociology was embedded in religion. Indeed, all of the human phenomena which are now the provinces of the various social sciences were in ancient times integrated around the prevailing conceptions of theology and morality.

We have not attempted to offer here a definition of money; in fact, we have often spoken of money ambiguously—as a symbol and as an institution. However, it would seem that one of the proper functions of money is to establish a communion through the communication of information concerning human emotional relationships. A good monetary institution should increase the well-being of the community and the happiness of its citizens, for it should provide a unit of accounting instead of a rough estimate of each individual's just apportionment of renunciations and gratifications. The good will of superiors and colleagues wavers, and political fortunes fluctuate. Memory is fickle, unreliable, and subject to unconscious biases; and people die or move away, leaving behind no record of a person's accomplishments or evil deeds. For these reasons, the merits of an individual tend to be forgotten over periods of time, or various passions interfere with accurate recollections and evaluations. With the appearance of a unit of account, everyone stands a better chance of receiving justice. Money is an objectification of numerous human memories, functioning to preserve human rights through the years, and thereby promoting basic emotional security within each individual.

The advent of electronic data-processing, as we have previously indicated, provides powerful new tools for the promotion of justice to all people in an industrialized world consisting of the interrelated activities of billions of people. Of course, mechanized systems for the evaluation of individuals' merits and needs will perhaps always retain crudities resulting from the difficulty of quantifying our mental, emotional, and social life; so that the effectiveness of a good monetary institution will at all times require the efforts of people of sensitivity, intelligence, and higher dedication. However, it is largely through relative price and wage levels that modern economic justice is administered, and high-speed record-keeping and decision-making machines will surely offer more and more rational methods for the establishment of these ratios. Prices and wages ultimately reduce to individual efforts and renunciations within social groups, and it is the function of money, in whatever symbolic form it may take, to control and regulate these efforts and renunciations in accordance with human values.

5. THE QUEST FOR GRACE

The attainment of a high level of production and consumption of material goods does not in itself constitute a sufficient condition for the welfare of humanity. If our incentives to work and consume become solely hedonistic pleasure, coupled with the desire to take revenge upon others by some form of ostentation, we place ourselves upon an exhausting, never-ending, and ungratifying treadmill turning ever faster and less purposively.

It is only by actualizing the higher potentialities symbolized by money that justice can be secured within large organizations and emotional fulfillment restored to our producing and consuming activities. To do so, we must attain the insight and the courage to think of money in its true sense, as a symbol of grace.

According to the viewpoints proposed in this book, man's deepest happiness stems from his identification with the creative energies of nature, whereby the individual dedicates himself to the advancement of civilization. Grace may therefore be construed as the awakening within a person of this insight into his real nature. Grace is divine inspiration.

The utopian, or holy organization is constituted by the mutual identification of its members with the divine powers. It is composed, in other words, of those individuals who have received grace. Insofar as money symbolizes sincere devotion to work, it expresses the divine inspiration. In this ideal sense, receiving money is a type of initiation ceremony, in which the individual renews his creative joy in the actualization of his potentialities.

Because of the cynicism of modern times, these statements of ethical idealism tend to be debunked. However, while a certain degree of cynicism is perhaps healthy, at the same time the source of life inspiration and moral vigor should not be ignored. Laum[14] has emphasized the emotional vitality of economic rootedness in the folk societies of the past, and Stanley Edgar Hyman suggests that money symbolism be restored to its folk significance in terms of such categories as "the hero, ritual communion, the cycle of the year as a pattern of life related to the earth, the symbols of worship, and the dignity of occupation."[15] What is needed, in Wolfgang Köhler's phrase,[16] is to "debunk the debunkers."

Acting in accordance with these ideals requires strength and integrity. For the possession of money often produces acceptance by the community, regardless of whether or not it was earned by making some genuine contribution to human welfare. Receiving money is for many people necessary to gratify their craving for status, and they care little about whether they deserved this recognition.

In a sensate culture, money is thus often a symbol of false values which tend to engulf all members of the society into the attitudes of avarice, malice, and hedonism, and which tend to obliterate the meaning of money as a symbol of grace. The monetary institution first manifested the highest ideals of the ancient Graeco-Roman culture, ideals which many centuries later found expression in the formation of the traditions of the United States. In its finest significance, money was a covenant among inspired individuals devoted to a great cause, such as the Declaration of Independence:

". . . And for the support of this declaration, with a firm reliance on the protection of Divine Providence, we mutually pledge to each other our lives, our fortunes, and our sacred honour."

PART 6

Further Speculations on the
Significance of Ancient Money

thirteen

A FREUDIAN INTERPRETATION OF EARLY MONEY

1. THE PSYCHOPATHOLOGY OF MONEY

It is reported that the 200,000,000 sacred cattle in India consume three times as much food as the hungry, often starving populace. This appears to be an instance in which religious ideas express ignorance and immaturity, and encourage backwardness and hardship. As in a neurosis, this practice seems to be symptomatic of tenaciously held images which are detrimental to the individual's development. If we were able to be present at the animal sacrifices of ancient Greece and Rome, we might find it equally difficult to discern any noble ideals amid the nauseating stench of the slaughterhouse which was the center of the archaic religion.

The Freudian oriented reader has no doubt already made many interpretations of the food rituals from which ancient money originated. Professor Martin P. Nilsson, one of the leading authorities on early Greek religion, says that the Freudian interpretation of Greek myths has, in spite of its exaggerations, yielded in instances a deep understanding.[1]

Psychopathology must be considered within the context of the gradual growth in the capacity for mature living. Just as the aim of psychoanalysis and psychiatry is to produce health, so the purpose of a social institution is to establish a fertile environment for the unfolding of human potentialities. Our investigation of the origin of money may be conceived as an exploration of the repressed love, hatred, and fear in our culture, our objective being to understand these forces and to utilize this knowledge for the betterment of man.

The psychopathology of money results from the carrying-over of infantile or adolescent motivations into adult life. In this respect, we might liken the sacred meal from which money arose to a fraternity dinner dance after a college football game. Indeed, the pleasures of the feast, preceded by the joy of combat and the triumph of the victor, and followed by love-making, seem to be a universal pattern in social life. Such festivities were originally religious rituals, and the very word "holiday" stems from "holy day." In the earliest times, we have reason to believe that these sacred occasions were often in the nature of meat orgies and sexual revelries following the killing of the old king and the accession of the new ruler to the crown. If we pursue these customs further, along the lines of Freud's theories, we find that the holy feast of the brothers was originally, either actually or symbolically, a cannibalistic meal stemming from a primeval Oedipal situation.

The campus festivities in fact are the typical activities of the uninitiated youths awaiting their examination ordeal by the elders before being accepted as mature contributors to the work life of the society. As such, the social occasions of undergraduate days often reflect the difficulties and anxieties of the adolescent about to enter into the world of adults. The struggle for grades, the demands of the parents, the feelings of inferiority, the sorrows of unrequited love, the competition for eminence, and the sexual gropings all tend to be bound up in the traditional rites of the college.

The role of the Greek-letter society in the development of some individuals is in some respects analogous to the part played by the ancient city in the history of the culture, in that both represent an intermediary point between the organization of life within kinship patterns and the emergence of the mass urban association of strangers. It is when the immature aspects of kinship relations fail to be abandoned in favor of more rational interests that we encounter the abnormal functioning of money in the life of the individual and of the culture. Initiation into the modern monetary institution, like the primitive puberty ordeal, often presents challenges and difficulties, right or wrong, which many persons are unable to face, and it is here that we encounter, from the standpoint of the individual, the psychopathology of money.

The origin of all of these life problems, according to many psychoanalysts, is the trauma of birth, and it may well be that this painful and overwhelming separation of child from mother is at the core of all later anxieties pertaining to money, for it is here that everyone first experiences the feeling of being lost or abandoned. The loss of the support supplied by the maternal womb against the force of gravity is perhaps the source of the irrational fear of the loss of financial support against the unfeeling demands of economic efficiency in adult life. To the extent that this is the case, the acquisition of money expresses an unconscious urge to overcome the trauma of birth by finding a mother substitute which provides an infallible supply of emotional security. Modern institutions such as our giant insurance companies and corporations would thus represent on a depth level the figure of a great protective maternal parent. The architecture of many bank buildings directly stems from the style of the ancient temples, which were the abode of the parental images. Speculating still further, we might conjecture that aspects of the birth trauma inhere in the irrational features of financial panics such as bank runs.

If we pursue the line of thought that the desire to obtain money basically represents the wish to remain in the infantile state of nondifferentiation from the mother, we must next consider the oral stage of libidinal development, during which the child feels itself to be in a deep sentimental union with its mother. Nursing at the mother's breast is an act of love; and, since the child is completely dependent upon the mother at this time, it develops the image of a protective helper who can be absolutely trusted and relied upon. Identification with the maternal figure occurs through suckling, which is psychically equivalent to an oral incorporation. Money, which indeed originated in the obtaining and distribution of food, thus symbolizes mother's milk and the emotional complexities associated with breast feeding.

To some extent, then, we may suppose that the participation in the communion symbolized by the early monetary forms represented the psychic attainment of an identification with the mother image. This is particularly evident in the function of ancient money as a fetish, or magical amulet, by means of which omnipotence and libidinal gratification were obtained from the mother goddess of fertility. Quite likely such motivations exist in the unconscious mind of modern man. It is a good guess that irresponsibility in borrowing and repaying money can often be traced to the manner in which an individual was breast-fed and weaned. The psychology of the spendthrift, the miser, the lazy unemployable, and the shirker is known to be frequently related to early maternal relationships. Psychoanalysts are well acquainted with the difficulties of the overprotected child in earning money in a world he is completely unprepared to face.

We have not discovered any information pertaining to ancient anal practices related to money.

Further symbolic qualities of money may perhaps be adduced from the work of Melanie Klein on the pregenital development of the libido. According to this psychoanalyst, when the mother absents herself from the baby, the child reacts with rage, and seeks cannibalistically to incorporate the mother to prevent any such future separation. The hostile component of this oral wish causes the infant to feel guilty, and fear of the mother's retaliation and fantasies of restitution for these destructive desires become important factors in the development of the child's personality.

Melanie Klein's point of view suggests that early money may have symbolized these oral aggressions against the mother. We often hear in the business world of a person "living off the fat of the land" and of a superior "chewing up" a subordinate. The big cigar clenched in the teeth is one of the stereotypes of the "bloated" financier. In business negotiations, as in poker, a frequent technique is to manipulate the other's anxieties, and there is no question but that unconscious masochistic and sadistic tendencies play an important part in financial dealings. Possibly these factors enter into price formation in the competitive market. Certainly feelings of dependency, lack of self-confidence, and the absence of fortitude are of considerable significance in the psychology of bargaining. Guilt feelings toward the mother, and the desire to make restitution very likely enter into the charitable bequests made by the wealthy, just as in ancient times this ambivalence may have been manifested in the vast pilgrimages to make votive offerings at the shrine of a mother goddess.

The sacrificial systems of antiquity were probably motivated to a great extent by internal tensions set up by the superego. The identifications, or introjections of the parents, bring about the establishment of the superego, the child's conception of what it ought to be like. Parental demands set up deep-rooted expectations of receiving or losing love for the performance or nonperformance of certain actions.

The ancestral cult of ancient times, stemming from the worship of the souls of the dead parents, was largely the result of the outward projection of the memories of the dead father and mother. The sacrificial offering in this sense was the result of an individual's desire to please his parents and to make amends for any hostility which he possessed. Receiving the medal coin or the sacrificial flesh, on the other hand, was equivalent to receiving the esteem of the parent figures. The desire to acquire money was thus motivated by the wish to be loved by the father and mother. Such motivations are of course commonplace to modern psychoanalysis. Abraham, by the way, suggested that spending money in certain instances is a substitute for a libidinal interest in the parents.[2]

The expression of early sibling rivalries in adults' frantic quest to acquire money is also frequently encountered in mental and emotional disorders. The child hates and fears his siblings as rivals to his monopoly. If these intense feelings become deeply engrained, they tend to be carried over into adult life. The offering of votive objects and the receiving of the flesh at the sacrificial meal in the ancient ancestral cults were to a great extent an expression of an immature need for fame. The jealousy, envy, and arrogance which were so disruptive of harmonious social organization no doubt were also strongly motivated by emotional fixations upon parental love. The irrational quest for grace—the desire to become one of the "elect"—was probably often the expression of the desire on the part of the quarreling siblings to be the most favored by the father and mother; and enthusiasm, in its infantile aspect, was the individual's feeling that he had received this special blessing.

In a phallic sense, we may regard money as having the significance of an initiation, or puberty ritual. One of the marks of having entered manhood for the modern youth is earning money, just as in ancient times receiving a share in the sacrificial flesh was a sign of an adolescent's being accepted as a mature member of the phratry. The payment of money may be conceived as a type of *rite de passage*—the entrance of an individual into a different sphere of community life. Our modern bureaucracies, with their graduated pay scales and status hierarchies, are to be compared with primitive secret societies in which a person rises in the tribal power structure through a series of initiations.

The making of money is thus symbolic of having "proved oneself": not to have amassed a large sum of money is to have, in an irrational sense, "failed." From an Adlerian point of view, the pathology of money could be regarded as stemming from an individual's need to compensate for inferiority feelings. The sense of power obtained from money would make up for early experiences of inadequacy resulting from organ inferiority; and, as a storehouse of social esteem, money would cause a person to feel that he is not being neglected. Money also enables a person to become a center of attention, in the manner of a spoiled, demanding child.

2. THE COMPULSIVE QUEST FOR MONEY

Certainly for many individuals earning and saving money is an attempt to overcome inner doubts as to their sexual potency. Possibly for such persons receiving a *salary* is, both from an etymological and a psychoanalytic point of view, equivalent to obtaining more salt, i.e., more sexual energy. For many people, money (or the consumer goods it can buy) functions as a type of medal which enables them to show off before the members of the opposite sex. Expensive female attire, for example, might to a large extent be regarded as a magical charm which it is hoped will act in the manner of an aphrodisiac.

Motivations concerning money are obviously closely linked with an individual's sexual life.* Husbandry, the providing for a wife and family, of course necessitates making a living. Winning a mate and the desire to adorn her also spur a person to acquire money. It would seem that the need to appear power-ful, hence attractive, to women, is another such motivation; it

---

* The influence of the monetary institution upon marriage and family structure is beyond the scope of this essay.

may be that money often functions as a symbol or fetish unconsciously representing strength and sexual gratification. In such instances, the quest for money may be an obsessive form of behavior stemming from repressed Oedipal desires.

The trauma of the Oedipus situation results from the rivalry between father and son for the love of the mother. The son hates his father, and fears him as a dangerous rival. A conflict of ambivalence results from the wish for the death of a beloved parent. The overwhelming guilt and fear arising from these feelings cause a repression of the desire to possess the mother and kill the father. In the course of normal development, the child eventually gives up the mother as a love object, attaching his libido to other objects. Repressed incestuous desires may also be sublimated into cultural activities. In the resolution of the Oedipus situation, the child abandons the desire for omnipotence stemming from the original dual unity with the mother.

When the unconscious desire to possess the mother and kill the father is not abandoned or sublimated, the Oedipus complex develops, and the repressed impulses are forced to express themselves through substitute or disguised gratifications. These gratifications are not of a mature nature and are fixed upon objects or events which, through unconscious associations, stem from incestuous desires. The hatred of the father may be displaced upon substitute objects, such as people in authority, while the love for the mother may be irrationally transferred to other women or upon objects or activities associated with early maternal fixations. The libido may regress to earlier developmental stages, such as the oral or anal, and to magical activities for recapturing the original feeling of omnipotence experienced in the arms of the mother.

The compulsion neurosis stems from the return of the repressed impulses to possess the mother and kill the father. The individual becomes obsessed by irrational thoughts or interests which cannot be understood since their psychic source is forcibly excluded from consciousness.

It seems likely that an intense drive to acquire money often stems from Oedipal motivations. In such cases, the love of money would be the expression of repressed incestuous desires. This hypothesis would explain the never-ceasing drive to make more and more money, far beyond the individual's needs, a motivation which we frequently encounter in contemporary life.

The earning of money not only represents the acquisition of an unconscious love object, but also enables a person to identify with his father, for money brings power and status in the community, and is a major source of strength in the world of commerce. An aggressive businessman may often be an individual who needs to attack and overpower a financial father figure. The Oedipal battle between father and son for possession of the mother may thus be transferred into the battle for power within the market or within the bureaucracy, with money as the symbol of victory.

The obsessive act may also represent a reaction against repressed hostility. The feeling of guilt toward the father may cause an individual to seek to "prove himself" in his professional or business activities, in this way "undoing" his unconscious hostility and incestuous desires. As Max Weber has shown, earning money is for many individuals a sign of grace—that is to say, a mark of having been saved rather than damned. By working hard and saving money, the person seeks to overcome his feeling of sinful worthlessness, i.e., tries to make atonement for his Oedipal guilt. In this respect, receiving money is a type of ritual whereby the individual cleanses himself of guilt, in a manner comparable to the purificatory rituals of the ancient religions. Work inhibitions and pathological boredom and inertia may result from guilt stemming from a person's unconscious feeling that in competing he is being hostile to his father.

3. TOTEMISM

The intense, widespread need to acquire more and more money suggests that this behavior is part of a mass obsessional neurosis. According to Freud's *Totem and Tabu* hypothesis, the animal sacrifice, from which ancient coinage arose, stemmed from a primordial Oedipus situation. This theory is extremely speculative, and has been rejected by most anthropologists; it was, however, accepted by Jane Harrison, one of the leading scholars in ancient Greek religion.[3]

Freud's hypothesis sought to explain the origin of one of man's first religious beliefs, totemism, as well as the origin of the law against incest, a tabu which in primitive cultures is often closely associated with totemic ideas.

Totemism, a form of religion found among numerous primitive cultures, consists of the veneration of certain environmental objects, usually an animal or plant. The group of people worshiping a totem consider themselves as descended from this animal or plant, which they regard as their protector and leader. The clan, phratry, or tribe and the members of these groups take the name of the totem, and pictures of the totem are often used as coats of arms; on certain religious occasions the skin of the totem animal is worn.

Totemism is also associated with two important laws: the prohibition against killing and eating the totem; and the prohibition against marrying a member of the same totemic group. Thus, totemism is intimately connected with the law of exogamy, i.e., the incest tabu. At certain holy rites, these two basic laws of totemism are broken; and in killing and eating the totem animal, the primitives believe that they are magically identifying themselves with this divinity. The sacrificial meal of antiquity, it was suggested by Robertson Smith, originated in totemic rites.*

According to the French sociologist-philosopher, Emile Durkheim, totemic symbols and rites are expressions of the moral consciousness of the group. The totemic symbol is a representa-

---

* Actually, the nature of totemism has been disputed, and all of the above characteristics of totemism are not encountered in many of the cultures in which totemic features have been found. Robertson Smith's theory was not accepted.

tion of the tradition of the community—it is a memorial of the soul of the ancestors. These symbols, displayed on sacred occasions, serve to reaffirm the social cohesion of the community by inspiring the members of the group to identify with the immortal heroes whose deeds comprise the history of the community. In wearing the skin of the totem animal, or by using images of the totem animal as heraldic devices, the primitive believes himself to be magically identified with his community. The director of the rituals—the priest—often dons a garment which represents, wholly or partially, the body of the totem animal; in this way, the religious leader personifies the tradition of the group. The fact that the totem animal represents the community explains why its image is frequently used as the coat-of-arms of the group.[4]

4. FREUD'S HYPOTHESIS

Totem and Tabu is based upon the suggestion originally made by Charles Darwin and later adopted by Atkinson[5] that man first lived in small groups consisting of a single powerful male who gathered around himself as many females as he could, driving off any other males who approached his horde. When his sons reached puberty, a struggle would take place for supremacy, ending in most instances with the killing or explusion of the sons.

According to this theory, one day the sons who had been outlawed from the horde by the jealous sire banded together and killed the father, after which, in order to acquire his strength and potency, they ate his body. Freud assumes that this band of brothers were ambivalent toward the murdered father: they loved the patriarch, and felt remorse after having committed the "primal crime." They also feared that the father's soul would return to punish the perpetrators of the murder.

As in the case of modern neurotics, the fear and guilt felt

toward the father was manifested in a desire to "undo" the dreadful deed by "subsequent obedience" to the commands of the patriarch. This was one of the motivations which led to establishing the incest tabu. An additional reason for the formation of the law of exogamy was the desire to avoid continual jealous rivalries and fighting by prohibiting all of the brothers from having sexual relations with any of the women of the horde.

The ambivalence toward the father was displaced on to an animal, toward which all of the attitudes now felt toward the murdered father were expressed. This animal became the totem. Like the actual father, it was regarded as the ancestor of the group and as a protector and leader. Identification with the totem animal by wearing its skin and by using its picture as a coat-of-arms resulted from the fact that the animal was a father substitute. The two basic laws of totemism were created by the subsequent obedience of the sons to the father's commands: the animal could not be killed and eaten (as had been the case with the father); and it was forbidden to marry another individual descended from the same totem.

The totem feast held on high religious holidays had two motivations: on the one hand, it was a repetition of the original parricide, whereby the sons' hostility was again expressed by the killing and eating of the animal; and, secondly, it was an attempt to propitiate the father by offering him a sacrifice. In this ritual, the entire community was required to share in the guilt by being present at the slaughter of the victim, and by eating a portion of the sacrificial flesh.

Man's first religion, totemism, thus resulted from the guilt of the sons toward the father, whom they killed in order to gratify their incestuous desires. Later religions had as their central aim the reconciliation of the ambivalence between father and son. In the totem feast, which was continued in the animal sacrifice and the public meals of classical antiquity, the primal crime was repeated by the killing and eating of the victim, in this way simultaneously expressing the son's triumph over the father, along with repentence.

5. THE BULL AS FATHER IMAGE

The psychoanalyst Flügel has compared regicide with parricide, pointing out the similarity between the killing of the king and the Oedipal conflict.[6] Each slaying of the king can be conceived as a repetition of the primal crime. As the physical strength and potency of the king waned, the son, gaining in courage, would challenge the father-king to a contest for the kingship. There is considerable evidence that these brutal struggles have recurred throughout the history of mankind.

The father was the fertility spirit, and, as provider of food, leader of food-obtaining activities, and magical producer of crops, he embodied the vital powers of nature which cause all living things to multiply and to grow. The struggle was hence between the old and new fertility spirit. Victory for the son meant obtaining the leadership of the family group and its food-producing activities—control over mother-earth: killing the king-father to assure the fertility of the crops was part of the Oedipal conflict.

Possibly in the course of the centuries this grim cycle of repeated parricide was abated by permitting the king to reign for a stated number of years before being killed and succeeded in office. Eventually the sacrificial victim was substituted for the father. The sacred bull of ancient times was such a father image. Both in Canaanite and Cretan mythology a bull god mated with the mother goddess.[7] Jane Harrison wrote:

> In Crete we have the worship of the Mother and the Child . . . we have also the theriomorph, the holy Bull, the "horns of consecration"; we cease to wonder that the Cretan palace is full of bulls and horns, we cease to wonder at the story of Pasiphaë and the Minotaur. In Asia Minor, in Phrygia, the same conjunction, the Mother and the Child and the Bull; in Thrace, in Macedon, in Delphi, in Thracianized Thebes again the same.[8]

In some instances the bull was regarded as a son god. This occurred, according to Freud, when, in the later development of religion, the son releases the other brothers from their sense of guilt by himself becoming the sacrificial victim. At the same time, however, the son achieves his original goal: as a god, he now attains the prerogatives of the father.[9]

The tender aspect of the brother symbolism of the bull resulted from the mutual identification of each individual with the beloved parent image. This is illustrated in the Mithraic religion. However, the bull sacrifice also expressed hostility stemming from rivalries among the brothers for the dominant, paternal position in the group.

6. ELATION AND MELANCHOLIA
IN THE ANIMAL SACRIFICE

Freud acknowledged in *Totem and Tabu* that he had not adequately accounted for the primitive mother goddesses. The study of these maternal deities might well lead to a deeper psychic level in the origin of law and religion, that of love, dependency, hostility, and guilt toward the mother. The totem animal may have partially represented a maternal image. In his study of the Mentaweian culture, Muensterberger found that the sacrificial animal symbolized the ambivalence toward both the father and mother.[10] The sacrifice was an expression of aggression, followed by a tabu period of remorse and obsessive efforts to overcome guilt.

The bull sacrifice may thus have represented hostility toward both the father and mother, along with the tender desire to incorporate and identify with the loved objects. Eating a portion of the sacrificial flesh unconsciously symbolized receiving milk from the breast, incest with the mother, and the killing and eating of the father. At the same time, the totem feast may have been an obsessive act in which the communicants sought to make expiation to the god and goddess. The bull as a parent symbol is often encountered in patients' dreams.[11] Various psychoanalysts have noted that the eating of food may be unconsciously equated with cannibalism, particularly with eating

the parents.[12] Abnormal elation has been traced to the influence
of early breast-feeding activities.[13] According to Freud, the in-
ternalization of a lost love object in cannibalistic fantasies
enables the individual to assuage his grief through identification.[14] Feelings of guilt, atonement, and forgiveness in an adult
may be a repetition of the childhood situation of wakening rage,
hunger, return of the mother, and blissful nursing at the
breast.[15]

Fluctuations in group psychology between melancholia and
elation are also influenced by the varying relation of the group
to its god (in this context, the outwardly projected superego).
When a member of the group fails to obey the commands of the
internalized parent, he experiences guilt, or melancholia. By
re-establishing himself in the grace of the deity through the
sacrifice, he places himself in communion with the god. In the
festivals of ancient Greece this identification with the deity was
consummated in the eating of his body in the form of the king
or bull.

7. TOTEMIC SURVIVALS
IN ANCIENT GREECE

Scholarship is divided on the question of the survival of
totemism in ancient Greece. In his authoritative work on
Greek religion, Martin P. Nilsson states that all attempts to
prove this hypothesis have been fruitless.[16]

Some scholars, however, have supported the theory, two of
the earliest having been Andrew Lang and McLennan. Farnell
regarded certain ancient Greek sacrificial communion rituals
as containing traces of an earlier totemic period.[17] A. B. Cook
regarded as totemic survivals the various animal cults in
which the participants dressed themselves as animal gods in
order to symbolize their relationship to these deities.[18] George
Thomson states that totemism survived in ancient Greek religion, and regards the Roman *gens* as having originated in

totemic clans.[19] Jane Harrison was of the opinion that a form of totemism expressed itself in Greek religion.[20]

There is considerable evidence for totemic survivals in early Greek dramatic presentations. It is well known to all historians of the theater that the tragedy arose from the rites of Dionysus, who was represented as a bull or a goat, and whose skin was worn by his worshipers.[21] It is likely that in pre-Greek religions an important part was played by masked men imitating animal-headed deities.[22] Cook gives many examples of priests and priestesses bearing animal titles.[23]

Initiation ceremonies in ancient Greece show striking similarities to the totemic rites of primitive communities. This has been commented upon by such writers as Hutton Webster, Andrew Lang, Van Gennep, and particularly Jane Harrison.

Numerous scholars have traced the origin of higher aspects of ancient Greek culture to magic rituals and religious practices similar to those found in primitive cultures. Francis Macdonald Cornford traced Attic comedy to primitive ritual forms, and advanced the hypothesis that the Olympic Games had a similar origin; he also showed that many of the conceptions of Greek philosophy originated in primitive beliefs such as are found in totemism.

A holy goat was often sacrificed to Athena, and it seems likely that her statue was sometimes wrapped in the *aegis,* or goat-skin.[24] The *Iliad* occasionally refers to the deities in animal form, as for example: "And Athena withal and Apollo of the silver bow, in the likeness of vulture birds, sate them upon a tall oak holy to aegis-bearing Zeus."

Jane Harrison regarded the bull rites of ancient times as totemic in character. Frazer admitted the possibility of such an interpretation; but because the existence of totemism among the early Greeks and Romans had not been established, he placed more weight upon the conservative interpretation of the bull as a vegetation deity.[25]

8. TOTEMIC SYMBOLS ON COIN TYPES

The possibility of a totemic origin of the animal images on Greek coins was advanced as early as McLennan.[26] Cook advanced a similar hypothesis, citing numerous examples of animal gods on Greek coins:

> Another trace of primitive skin-wearing is to be found in the numismatic symbols of certain cities. Just as the warrior adopted the animal-garb for his armorial bearings, so the community to which he belonged took it for their monetary token. . . .
>
> Finally, a community which adopted as its badge the symbol of the animal that it worshiped, would not be unlikely to call itself by that animal's name. It is in this way that we should probably explain the animal titles attached to certain early Greek townships and tribes . . .[27]

D. P. Costello also suggests that the coats-of-arms of certain Athenian clans may be the survivals of the old totems.[28]

Jean B. Cammann has discussed the fact that the symbols on many ancient coins pertain to various legends contained in Greek mythology.[29] This work does not consider the possibility of a totemic origin for these myths. However, students of mythology have found that myths often stem from early ritual sources. Hence it may be that the mythic symbols on Greek coins are traceable to primitive totemic ceremonies. We might also refer here to a parallel among the Northwest American Indians, where heraldic crests of a totemic nature were highly prized as status symbols, and played an important part in ceremonials.

9. THE PSYCHOANALYSIS OF MONEY

If the sacrificial practices and the symbols on coins in ancient times can be regarded in some sense as totemic survivals, then a Freudian interpretation of the early forms of money as signifying Oedipal and pregenital complexes can be ventured. Some of the findings of psychoanalytic writers, such as G. Pederson-Krag,[30] Gorer,[31] and Bergler,[32] on modern attitudes toward money would seem to add weight to such viewpoints. Research on ulcers and other psychosomatic disorders shows that the quest for money is often motivated by powerful unconscious needs stemming from infantile relations to the parents. The hypothesis that the first coins were medals suggests that the need to acquire money is closely associated with the body image; many primitive moneys, such as rings, are often worn as ornaments. Many of the theories advanced by psychoanalysts to explain modern attitudes toward money have tended to neglect sociological, economic, and political factors.[33] However, the neo-Freudian schools, particularly the followers of Fromm and Horney, have emphasized the influence of the culture on personality development and disorders.

It seems likely that underlying economic behavior are various unconscious attitudes which contribute to such mass crises as booms, panics, and depressions. Fluctuations in the market may be related to melancholia and elation in group psychology; in modern times, the economy tends to replace the fertility god as the source of the well-being of the community. More profound forces may, however, exert an unconscious determining influence upon economic life. Agnes Baldwin, a follower of Jung, has discussed the eucharistic symbols on ancient coins as expressing the transformation of psychic energy into a higher religious form.[34] The origin of coinage in ancient rituals, it is apparent, offers a rich and challenging field for further psychoanalytic study.

fourteen

MONEY AND THE MARKET ECONOMY

1. THE ORIGIN OF THE MARKET

The beginnings of coinage were closely associated with the emergence of the institution of the market. It was only with the dissolution of the household economy and the development of free buying and selling that these symbols could become the kind of circulating media of exchange that we now think of as money.

The point of view that ancient coinage arose from the state's effort to facilitate barter by affixing its seal upon a precious metal to guarantee its weight and purity results from the projection backward into antiquity of our modern commercial attitudes. The market is not an institution which naturally arises in all human societies, and there is reason to believe that the market institution did not exist in early Greece, but was a later development.[1] Primitives do not typically exchange goods by haggling over prices in a marketplace. On the contrary, economic interchange occurs within a complex texture of traditional kinship and ceremonial relations.[2] Practices such as the marriage gift, the *wergild* (blood money), and fines levied by the king play an important role in primitive economics. We do not aspire to discuss here the anthropological literature on this subject, but we shall offer some speculations as to possible future research on money and the market economy.[3]

The connection between the origin of markets and religious festivals is particularly striking in the medieval fairs, from which many of the great market centers arose. The pilgrim and the merchant were often one and the same person, the "company" (literally, "those who eat bread together") originating as a group of pious individuals journeying toward a holy sanctuary which was also a market.[4]

The German word *messe* means both "mass" and "fair"; and the term "fair" comes from the Latin *feria*, or holy day, which is derived from the same root as the word for "feast." Many of the German markets were closely associated in their origin with the festivals of saints, and it is likely that these are traceable to the great heathen sacrificial feasts held in the tribal holy places. In this connection, we can glimpse in our modern custom of exchanging gifts at Christmas the practice in pagan Europe of hanging votive offerings on a sacred tree. Many of the earliest markets in Britain and Ireland originated from pagan fairs or festivals connected with the worship of the dead. These feasts were held in cemeteries and in churchyards serving as burial places.[5] Market gods existed in early Britain, some named after Celtic divinities. The Penzance market cross, for example, was of pagan origin.

In Arabia and in India, fairs and markets often arose at the shrines of pilgrims. We see Mohammed delivering diatribes against the selling of goods at shrines by merchants, and we will remember the incident of Christ driving the money changers out of the Temple. In ancient times, the gatherings at Teuta, in the Egyptian delta, were given over both to religion and the exchange of goods. Theophrastus states that a priest of the Temple of the Sun permitted trade in the Temple itself, and collected the dues on behalf of the divinity. Pausanias tells of a similar practice at a fair held near the shrine of Isis.

Markets in early Greece were connected with the worship of the dead. Pausanias gives many examples of markets being held near the graves of dead heroes. For example, the market place at Megara was held at the ancient grave of Coroebus. The Roman market day was celebrated with great banquets, and was dedicated to Jupiter by the sacrifice of a bull.[6] Many ancient writers held that these market days were *feriae,* feast days.[7] The market in Athens originated in the agora, and in Rome in the forum, and these public areas were also places of religious assembly.

Laum discussed the age-old connection between the market and religious festivals in many lands, and pointed to the close association of the market and religious cult in ancient Greece and Rome.[8] It is well known that the great religious gatherings in early Greece were also important marketplaces, and that special coins were often struck at these festivals for distribution among the pilgrims.

Various hypotheses have been offered to account for these facts. The presence of a large number of people at a religious festival, it is asserted, provided traders with the opportunity to sell their wares. Another theory holds that trade in holy places resulted from the necessity of caring for the pilgrims. Still another hypothesis is that trading was facilitated by the sacred peace which was maintained at the place of religious festivals and on the roads leading to the shrine. Laum suggested that the existence of the market within the temple resulted from the efforts of the priests to trade surpluses resulting from votive offerings.

2. HOUSEHOLD ECONOMY AND MARKETPLACE

The development of a complete market economy did not take place in the ancient world, which remained largely a redistributive economy. It is apparent that the circulation of the cult symbols stemming from the animal sacrifice was part of a large sociological process in which the household economy underwent a transition to the marketplace.

The existence of a city requires some institution for the interchange of the goods and services produced by the urban population for the food raised on the surrounding land. Such an institution may have existed in the form of the sacrificial system in the temple. In any case, there apparently came to be people not attached to any household, who received their food through some other institutional arrangement. As we stated previously, the origin of coinage is closely associated with the first retailing of food. Exactly how these new developments came about is not known, and we can only speculate broadly upon these problems.*

It may be presumed that in antiquity the city economy was controlled by the temple authorities. Most economic activity was carried on in the patriarchal kinship group. Homer speaks of the fifty brothers and twelve sisters living under Priam's roof, along with their wives, husbands, and children. The starting point for industry, as Max Weber has said, was in the production for the needs of the household.[9] The very word "economics" originally meant, in ancient Greece, "the management of the household." Where industry in primitive cultures is carried on by units other than the household, it is generally within an institution modeled after the family, such as the clan or a magical fraternity.

---

* See our discussion in Chapter XIII, Section 3.

For example, the industrial associations, or corporations, in ancient Rome, called "colleges," were duplicates in every respect of the *gens*. An essential part of their religious constitution was a sacred meal, at which the *sportula* was often distributed.

> . . . every college was a great family. The community of crafts and interest replaced the blood bond, and the confrères had, like the family, their common cult, their common meal, their common sepulchre. We have seen that their religious or funeral festivities were those of families; like them, they celebrated the "kinship tie" and the cult of the dead. They wished, we have also seen, to repose one day in the same tomb or at least side by side; until that time, they sat at the same table in a common house.[10]

Early economic activity in Greece and Rome was thus carried on within the kinship group, or in an artificial extension of the family. But the temple originated simply as the paternal household, the father as priest presiding over the family rituals and administering over the production and distribution of the goods necessary for the welfare of the group. Economic activity was under the control of the priest (the father), and the distribution of goods took place in the temple (the household). The origin of banking is to be found in the Greek temples, which carried on numerous productive activities, and which loaned out money for overseas trading ventures.* The temple of Diana at Ephesus, for example, was a vast commercial enterprise as well as a center of pilgrimages from all parts of the world.

The fact that markets in ancient times were often in existence within the temples suggests that the market originated in the breakdown of the household mode of distribution within the religious body. Under the kinship type of economy, the contribution made by each individual to the temple household was probably fixed by custom. The first form of taxation was the

---

* The temple treasury originated in the *thesaurus*, or granary, containing, as its first form of capital, grain for redistribution when needed. This banking function was thus also a type of insurance operation, in that both functions were expressions of a loyal bond of individuals devoted to mutual aid.

sacrificial offering which the votary brought to the priestly authority. In the course of time, according to Laum, the bull came to be used as a unit of reckoning in the taxation or sacrifical system. The state economy, which was also a religious household, would largely consist, according to this line of thought, of the redistribution, in the form of sacrificial flesh, of the tithes, or votive offerings brought by the communicants. The term "liturgy" in ancient Greece signified an offering; the first form of charity was the distribution of the sacrificial flesh to all members of the cult community.

With the gradual transition from the redistribution-type economy to the market economy, we may presume, following the medieval analogy, that the religious authorities continued to control the exchange of goods. As is the case in most primitive markets, the exchange ratios were probably fixed by custom, regarded as sacred law. With the growth of the market, the notion of the sacred tax became transformed into the conception of price, and we may further speculate that the unit of value within the taxation-redistribution economy, namely the sacrificial bull, became the unit of value in the market economy, i.e., money. The writings of Aristotle indicate a shift in ancient Greece from the religious conception of money as a means for attaining a just distribution to the modern conception of money as simply a medium of exchange.[11]

3. THE SOCIOLOGY OF
THE MARKET ECONOMY

We may perhaps discern within these historical transformations an illustration of Maine's theory[12] of the shift from status to contract as the principle of the relation of the individual to the community. Participation in the sacrificial meal originally signified the commitment of the individual to a bond of loyalty with the other members of the group—the entering into a covenant with the deity. The original form of the oath consisted of enter-

ing into communion with the sacrificial animal.* In order for
a legal relation to exist between two people, they had to worship
at the same hearth and perform the same sacrifices. Business
organizations originated as religious brotherhoods.[13] When two
people had not shared the same religious communion, no legal
relation could exist between them. "Law was nothing more than
one phase of religion. Where there was no common religion,
there was no common law."[14]

The particular portion of the sacrificial flesh which the communicant received, and his physical juxtaposition to the other
citizens at the feast signified his status in the community—his
standing. With the transition to the money economy, status
would be determined by the contractual relation between individuals. The two essential requirements for a legal contract—
an offer and an acceptance—were originally, we may conjecture,
the votive offering and the share in the sacrificial flesh. The
establishment of a contractual relationship between two individuals would thus retain traces of the original bond of religious
loyalty among members of the same communion, with impersonal
bargaining beginning to replace the patriarchal redistribution of
goods among the brotherhood. The persistence of the cult ritual
in the commercial agreement perhaps resulted from the survival
of the conviction that moral ideals (embodied in religious belief) should govern economic relations. The first magistrates and
lawyers were the priestly authorities, and we may presume that
these religious officers continued to regulate the exchange of
goods long after the breakdown of the household-type economy.

Pursuing these speculations further, we may suggest, on the
analogy of Max Weber's work,[15] that, with the establishment of
the market economy, the quest for grace, originally symbolized
by the cult symbols, would tend to become transformed into the

---

* The word "vote" is etymologically related to the Latin *votum*, the
votive offering or vow. This suggests that the political action of voting
originated as a pledge of support, or oath of allegiance. Both the political
contract and the commercial contract probably stemmed from participation
in the sacrificial meal, which established an individual in an indissoluble
communion with his fellows.

quest for money. With the decay of the sense of values based on genuine religious feeling, the possession of money would tend to be regarded as a social honor, regardless of whether or not the individual had made a worthwhile contribution to the welfare of the community. The sacred premonetary token, symbolizing the aristocrat's distribution of the share in the sacrificial bull flesh, gradually would come to circulate among the landless commercial classes, thereby enabling them to emulate their "pecuniary betters" by accumulating money (grace). At the same time, land, formerly a sacred, inalienable possession, entered into the market as a good to be bought and sold, thereby uprooting many individuals from their traditional ties. The self-esteem of individuals would tend to become increasingly dependent on the vicissitudes of the market. This legal change brought about economic insecurities and spiritual loneliness which facilitated the growth of tyranny in the ancient city. These anxieties no doubt contributed in part to the "failure of nerve" among the people of antiquity.[16]

4. THE GROWTH OF FREEDOM
WITHIN THE MARKET ECONOMY

At the same time, however, the breakdown of the old aristocracies freed men from paternalism, and gave rise to the ideal of democracy. The increasing political power of individuals of money caused an increase in vertical mobility, thus making it possible for many deserving individuals to be justly rewarded for their social contributions. Decisions concerning the production and distribution of the goods necessary for the welfare of the community, formerly made by the priestly authorities, were now increasingly the result of the bargaining of buyers and sellers. The rise of the market economy alienated man from his instruments of production, provided the opportunity for gain by financial manipulation, and replaced religious values by the cruel impersonality of the laws of supply and demand. However, the ability to contract freely probably tended to render economic decisions more democratic, more rational, and less subject to the stifling of individual initiative and the dominance of corrupt authority. Possibly much of the hostility toward the economic decisions of the authorities was now expressed in bargaining.

With rational reflection superseding ancestral custom, countless new freedoms opened in human relations and in the arts and philosophy. The basis for social organization—law—became gradually the subject of reasonable consideration, rather than a body of unalterable codes mystically derived by a special group of exegetes. This atmosphere of democracy and freedom gave rise to the great intellectual and spiritual tradition which produced modern science and civilization.

The money economy freed the individual from the dominance of the patriarchal authority, and enabled him to seek self-actualization through personal relationships of his own choosing. Man became increasingly at liberty to develop his own ethical ideals, and to live the good life as he saw fit. Freedom from ancestral tradition also facilitated the rise of higher religious ideals which insisted on loyalty to the universal brotherhood of man, rather than to the immediate kinship group. The growth of the market had a twofold effect: it destroyed man's feelings of emotional, economic, and spiritual security; but at the same time it established him as a rational person capable of free choice.[17] It is the great task of the twentieth century to frame institutions which will restore man's feeling of rootedness without sacrificing the integrity of the individual.

NOTES

Chapter one

1. Harry Scherman's *The Promises Men Live By* (New York: Random House, 1938) analyzes modern economic behavior into interpersonal promises and their fulfillment.

2. For a recent discussion of the point of view and findings of institutional economics see *Trade and Market in the Early Empires*, edited by Karl Polanyi, Conrad M. Arensberg, and Harry W. Pearson (New York: The Free Press and The Falcon's Wing Press, 1957).

3. The mathematical theory of strategy was developed by John von Neumann and Oskar Morgenstern in *Theory of Games and Economic Behavior* (Princeton University Press, 1947). There is now a large literature on this subject, but the best source for the nonmathematical layman is *Strategy in Poker, Business, and War*, by John McDonald (New York: W. W. Norton & Co., Inc., 1950).

4. Sigmund Freud, *Civilization and Its Discontents* (London: Hogarth Press, 1946), p. 83.

Chapter two

1. Jessie L. Weston, *From Ritual to Romance* (Garden City, N. Y.: Doubleday & Company, Inc., 1957).

2. Roger Sherman Loomis, *Arthurian Tradition and Chrétien de Troyes* (New York: Columbia University Press, 1949).

3. As Johannes Hasebroek has said, the ancient cities of Greece and Rome were ruled by aristocracies based "on force and unrestrained brutality." (*Trade and Politics in Ancient Greece* [London: G. Bell & Son, Ltd., 1933], pp. vii-viii.)

4. Audrey I. Richards, *Hunger and Work in a Savage Tribe* (New York: The Free Press, 1948), p. 14.

5. John A. Wilson, "Egypt," in *Before Philosophy*, by H. and H. A. Frankfort, John A. Wilson, and Thorkild Jacobsen (London: Penguin Books).

6. For example: L. Brillouin, "Life, Thermodynamics and Cybernetics," *American Scientist*, Vol. 37, No. 4 (October, 1949); Julian Huxley, "Evolutionary Humanism," *The Standard*, 39, No. 1 (October-November, 1952), 228; and Karl W. Deutsch, "Mechanism, Teleology, and Mind," *Philosophy and Phenomenological Research*, 12, No. 2 (December, 1951), 185-223.

7. Along the lines of modern information theory, we may say that an individual's "self" is an autonomous information network, capable of self-modification, which organizes the person's instincts. Since a pattern of information is independent of the particular physical form in which it exists, we may say that a given individual's personality is in a certain sense perpetuated so long as this organizational pattern is transmitted to another person. In this sense, even after we die, our "self" continues to exist in the form of those aspects of ourselves which we have contributed to the community. Each living individual is the temporary bearer of an information pattern, and is an agent of history, for his work tends to increase order and to decrease entropy.

8. Richards, *op. cit.*, p. 87.

Chapter three

1. Ferdinand Tönnies, *Fundamental Concepts of Sociology* (*Gemeinschaft und Gesellschaft*), translated and supplemented by Charles P. Loomis (New York: American Book Company, 1940), pp. 239-240.

2. Simone Weil, *The Need for Roots* (New York: G. P. Putnam's Sons, 1952), p. 98.

3. Josiah Royce, *The Problem of Christianity* (New York: Macmillan & Co., 1913).

4. Alfred North Whitehead, *Process and Reality* (New York: The Social Science Book Store, 1941).

5. See below, in this chapter, the section, "The Higher Significance of Phallic Symbols."

6. William McDougall, *The Group Mind* (2nd ed.; New York: G. P. Putnam's Sons, 1920), p. 8.

7. Sebastian De Grazia, *The Political Community* (The University of Chicago Press, 1948).

8. Lewis Richard Farnell, *The Higher Aspects of Greek Religion* (London: Williams & Norgate, 1921).

9. H. G. Baynes, *Mythology of the Soul* (London: Methuen & Co., Ltd., 1949), p. 460.

10. Farnell, *op. cit.*, p. 27.

11. The image of light or illumination is often found in religion and in literature as a symbol of the creative forces of life.

12. Ashley Montagu, *On Being Human* (New York: Henry Schuman, 1950).

13. Margaret Ribble, *The Rights of Infants* (Columbia University Press, 1943), pp. 4-7.

14. Ashley Montagu, *op. cit.*, p. 55.

15. *Ibid.*, p. 65.

16. Much work has been done on this subject from a psychoanalytic standpoint by Angel Garma, as for example, "On the Pathogenesis of Peptic Ulcer," *International Journal of Psycho-Analysis*, Vol. 31, Parts I and II, 1950.

17. Anthony M. Ludovici, *A Defense of Aristocracy* (London: Constable & Co., Ltd., 1915).

18. Erik H. Erikson, *Childhood and Society* (New York: W. W. Norton & Co., Inc., 1950).

19. Fustel de Coulanges, *The Ancient City*, translated by Willard Small (Boston: Lee and Shepard, 1874), p. 65.

20. "Phallism," in Hastings *Encyclopedia of Religion and Ethics*, Vol. 9, p. 829.

21. Jane Harrison, *Themis* (Cambridge at the University Press, 1927), p. 269.

22. *Ibid.*, p. 301.

23. *Ibid.*, p. 268.

24. James G. Frazer, *The Magic Art*, Vol. II (London: Macmillan & Co., 1926), p. 195.

25. J. Wilfrid Jackson, *Shells as Evidence of the Migrations of Early Culture* (Manchester at the University Press, 1917).

26. G. Elliot Smith, *The Evolution of the Dragon* (London: Longmans, Green & Co., 1919), p. 26.

Chapter four

1. Ernst Cassirer, *The Myth of the State* (New Haven: Yale University Press, 1946).

2. George Santayana, *The Life of Reason* (New York: Charles Scribner's Sons, 1948), p. 272.

3. Gilbert Murray, *Tradition and Progress* (Boston: Houghton Mifflin Co., 1922), p. 13.

4. Henri Bergson, *The Two Sources of Morality and Religion* (New York: Henry Holt & Co., 1935).

5. Bronislaw Malinowski, *Myth in Primitive Psychology* (London: Kegan Paul, 1926).

6. Leland P. Lovette, *School of the Sea: The Annapolis Tradition in American Life* (New York: Frederick A. Stokes Co., 1941), pp. 280-281.

7. Emile Durkheim, *The Elementary Forms of the Religious Life* (New York: The Free Press, 1947), p. 375.

8. A. R. Radcliffe-Brown, *Structure and Function in Primitive Society* (New York: The Free Press, 1952), p. 164.

9. President Truman's Foreword to *The Medal of Honor of the United States Army* (Washington: U.S. Government Printing Office, 1948), p. III.

Chapter five

1. The French historian Numa-Denys Fustel de Coulanges was born in Paris on March 18, 1830. Paul Guiraud, a biographer (*Fustel de Coulanges* [Paris: Librairie Hachette, 1896]) stated that his earlier works showed traces of a belief in necessary historical progress, but that by the time *La Cité Antique* was published (1864) this tendency had disappeared in favor of a strictly deterministic and empirical approach. Durkheim at one time studied under Fustel de Coulanges.

A. R. Radcliffe-Brown referred to *The Ancient City* as "a valuable contribution to the theory of the social function of religion" (*Structure and Function in Primitive Society,* [Glencoe: The Free Press, 1952], p. 161), but states that later research has indicated the necessity for some modifications in this work. In particular, he objects to conceiving religion as the sole determinant of the ancient society. Rather, he states, there was probably a causal interplay between religion and the other institutions of the cities of antiquity.

We shall regard ourselves in this essay as considering merely one determinant of the social structure of the ancient city. Other factors, such as geography and economics, were certainly present as important influences, but they will remain outside of our considerations. Max Weber discussed these in *General Economic History* (New York: The Free Press, 1950).

Henri Berr states in the Foreword to G. Glotz' *The Greek City* (London: Kegan Paul, 1929), p. xix, "the 'Cité Antique' must always be read because it embodies a large portion of the truth and because it is a remarkable piece of work, clear-cut and finished." Glotz refers to *The Ancient City* as a masterpiece; his criticisms are mainly on the ground that the development from family to phratry, tribe, and city did not occur in the orderly, logical fashion envisaged by Fustel de Coulanges.

Further criticisms of Fustel de Coulanges may be found in Ernst Cassirer's *The Problem of Knowledge* (New Haven: Yale University Press, 1950).

2. Fustel de Coulanges, *The Ancient City*, translated by Willard Small (Boston: Lee and Shepard, 1874), p. 23.

3. Hugh E. Seebohm, *On the Structure of Greek Tribal Society* (London: Macmillan & Co., 1895), p. 17.

4. Erich Fromm, *Man for Himself* (New York: Rinehart & Co., Inc., 1947), p. 159.

5. Bronislaw Malinowski said that primitive cultures with a closely knit family structure have the strongest chance to survive (*Freedom and Civilization* [New York: Roy Publishers, 1944], p. 117).

Chapter six

1. Bronislaw Malinowski, *Magic, Science, and Religion* (New York: The Free Press, 1948), p. 25.

2. Christopher Dawson, *Religion and Culture* (New York: Sheed & Ward, 1948), p. 139.

3. William Mitchell Ramsay, *The Church in the Roman Empire before A. D. 170* (New York: G. P. Putnam's Sons, 1893), p. 125.

4. James G. Frazer, *The Worship of Nature*, Vol. I (New York: The Macmillan Co., 1926), p. 320.

5. Percy Gardner, *The Types of Greek Coins* (Cambridge at the University Press, 1883), p. 174.

6. Martin P. Nilsson, *A History of Greek Religion* (Oxford at the Clarendon Press, 1949), p. 120. Also, Gilbert Murray, *Four Stages of Greek Religion* (New York: Columbia University Press, 1912), p. 34.

7. Lewis Richard Farnell, *The Cults of the Greek States*, Vol. I (Oxford at the Clarendon Press, 1896), p. 290.

8. *Ibid.*, Vol. II, p. 496.

9. *Ibid.*, Vol. III, p. 13.

10. Audrey I. Richards, *Hunger and Work in a Savage Tribe* (New York: The Free Press, 1948), p. 78.

11. Frazer, *op. cit.*, p. 44.

12. James G. Frazer, *Taboo and the Perils of the Soul* (London: Macmillan & Co., 1911), p. 1.

13. J. C. Flügel has discussed the transference of family attitudes to the state and to the state authorities. (*The Psycho-Analytical Study of the Family* [London: Hogarth Press, 1948], p. 127.)

14. Francis Macdonald Cornford, *The Origin of Attic Comedy* (Cambridge at the University Press, 1934), p. 19.

15. Ernst Curtius, *The History of Greece,* Vol. I (New York: Charles Scribner's Sons, 1902), p. 123.

16. Christopher Dawson, *The Age of the Gods* (London: John Murray, 1928), p. 361.

17. Lewis R. Farnell, "Sacrificial Communion in Greek Religion," (*The Hibbert Journal,* 2 [1903-4]), 306-322, 319.

18. Richard Thurnwald, *Economics in Primitive Communities* (Oxford at the University Press, 1932), p. 21.

19. W. Robertson Smith, *Lectures on the Religion of the Semites* (New York: D. Appleton & Co., 1889).

Chapter seven

1. James G. Frazer, *The Magic Art,* Vol. I (London: Macmillan & Co., Ltd., 1926), p. 420.

2. Sigmund Freud, *Totem and Tabu,* in *The Basic Writings of Sigmund Freud,* translated and edited by A. A. Brill (New York: The Modern Library, 1938).

Otto Fenichel, *The Psychoanalytic Theory of Neurosis* (New York: W. W. Norton & Co., Inc., 1945), p. 37.

Gardner Murphy, *Personality* (New York: Harper & Bros., 1947), p. 480.

Paul Schilder, *The Image and the Appearance of the Body* (London: Kegan Paul, 1935), p. 122.

3. Two excellent psychoanalytic papers on early mother goddesses are: Edith Weigert-Vowinkel's "The Cult and Mythology of the Magna Mater from the Standpoint of Psychoanalysis," *Psychiatry,* Vol. 1, No. 3; and Arun Kumar Ray Chaudhuri's "A Psycho-Analytic Study of the Hindu Mother Goddess (Kali) Concept," *The American Imago,* Vol. 13, No. 2.

4. Bronislaw Malinowski, *Coral Gardens and Their Magic,* Vol. I (London: George Allen & Unwin, Ltd., 1935), p. 77.

5. Christopher Dawson, *Religion and Culture* (New York: Sheed & Ward, 1948), p. 39.

6. Numerous illustrations are to be found in Frazer's *Spirits of the Corn and of the Wild,* Vol. II (London: Macmillan & Co., 1925).

7. Wilfred D. Hambly, *Source Book for African Anthropology,* Part II (Chicago: Field Museum of Natural History, Vol. 26 [1937]), p. 564.

8. Lewis R. Farnell, "Sacrificial Communion in Greek Religion" (*The Hibbert Journal,* 2 [1903-4]), p. 319.

Martin P. Nilsson, *A History of Greek Religion* (Oxford at the Clarendon Press, 1949), p. 58.

9. Bronislaw Malinowski, *Magic, Science, and Religion* (New York: The Free Press, 1948), p. 32.

10. "Cannibalism," in Hastings *Encyclopedia of Religion and Ethics,* Vol. 3, pp. 194-209.

11. Sir Paul Vinogradoff, *Outlines of Historical Jurisprudence,* Vol. I (New York: Oxford University Press, 1920), p. 352.

12. "Relics," in Hastings *Encyclopedia of Religion and Ethics,* Vol. 10, pp. 650-8.

13. Charles R. Beard, *Lucks and Talismans* (London: Sampson Low, Marston & Co., Ltd., 1934).

14. "Images and Idols (Greek and Roman)," Hastings *Encyclopedia of Religion and Ethics,* Vol. 7, p. 134.

15. James G. Frazer, *The Dying God* (London: Macmillan & Co., 1930), p. 202.

16. Sigmund Freud, "Mourning and Melancholia," *Collected Papers,* Vol. IV (London: The Hogarth Press, 1948), pp. 152-70.

17. George Frederick Kunz, *Rings for the Finger* (Philadelphia: J. B. Lippincott Co., 1917), p. 191.

18. "Regalia," Hastings *Encyclopedia of Religion and Ethics,* Vol. 10, p. 637.

19. Paul Einzig, *Primitive Money* (London: Eyre & Spottiswoode, 1949), p. 199.

Chapter eight

1. Arthur Evans, *Mycenaean Tree and Pillar Cult and Its Mediterranean Relations* (London: Macmillan & Co., 1901).

2. Edward B. Tylor, *Primitive Culture,* Vol. II (New York: Henry Holt & Co., 1874), p. 221.

3. Ernest H. Short, *A History of Religious Architecture* (London: Eyre & Spottiswoode, 1951).

4. Carl Boetticher, *Der Baumcultus der Hellenen* (Berlin: Weidmannsche Buchhandlung, 1856), p. 11.

5. James G. Frazer, *The Magic Art,* Vol. II (London: Macmillan & Co., 1926).

6. Arthur Bernard Cook, *Zeus,* Vol. III (Cambridge at the University Press, 1940), p. 314.

7. Arthur Bernard Cook, "The European Sky-God," *Folk-Lore* (December, 1904), pp. 369-426.

8. Arthur Bernard Cook, "Zeus, Jupiter, and the Oak," *Classical Review* (1903), pp. 174-186, 268-278, 403-421; (1904), pp. 75-89.

9. James G. Frazer, *Balder the Beautiful,* Vol. II (London: Macmillan & Co., 1923), p. 77.

10. Arthur Bernard Cook, *op. cit.,* Vol. I, pp. 86-87.

11. James G. Frazer, *Spirits of the Corn and of the Wild,* Vol. I (London: Macmillan & Co., 1925), p. 248.

12. "Sin-Eating," Hastings *Encyclopedia of Religion and Ethics,* Vol. 11, pp. 572-76.
13. William H. Desmonde, "The Bull-Fight as a Religious Ritual," *The American Imago,* Vol. 9, No. 20.
Jack Randolph Conrad, *The Horn and the Sword* (New York: E. P. Dutton & Co., Inc., 1957).

Chapter nine

1. Franz Cumont, *The Mysteries of Mithra* (Chicago: The Open Court Publishing Co., 1910).
2. James G. Frazer, *Spirits of the Corn and of the Wild,* Vol. I (London: Macmillan & Co., 1925), p. 16.
3. Jane Ellen Harrison, *Ancient Art and Ritual* (New York: Oxford University Press, 1948), p. 88.
4. Frazer, *op. cit.,* p. 17. The city cult did not, of course, take this ecstatic form.
5. Jane Ellen Harrison, *Prolegomena to the Study of Greek Religion* (Cambridge at the University Press, 1908), p. 481.
6. Royden Keith Yerkes, *Sacrifice in Greek and Roman Religions and Early Judaism* (New York: Charles Scribner's Sons, 1925), p. 108.
7. Lewis Richard Farnell, *The Cults of the Greek States,* Vol. V (Oxford at the Clarendon Press, 1909), p. 359.
8. Lewis Richard Farnell, "Magic and Religion in Early Hellenic Society," *Archiv für Religionswissenschaft,* Bd. 17 (1914), p. 27.
9. Henri Frankfort, *Kingship and the Gods* (The University of Chicago Press, 1948).
10. M. J. Herskovits, "The Cattle Complex in East Africa," *American Anthropologist,* 28 (new ser., 1926), 230-72, 361-88, 494-528, 633-64.
11. John Roscoe, *The Northern Bantu* (Cambridge at the University Press, 1915), p. 104.
12. Margaret Read, "Native Standards of Living and African Culture Change," *Africa* (Supplement), 11, No. 3 (1938), 5-56.
13. Otto Rank, *Art and Artist* (New York: Tudor Publishing Co., 1932), p. 132.
14. Wilfred D. Hambly, *Source Book for African Anthropology,* Part I (Chicago: Field Museum of Natural History, Vol. XXVI [1937]), p. 359.
15. Olaf Pettersson, *Chiefs and Gods* (Lund: C. W. K. Gleerup, 1953).

Chapter ten

1. A. R. Burns, *Money and Monetary Policy in Early Times* (London: Kegan Paul, 1927), pp. 6-8. According to William Ridgeway, the value

of gold, when it later came into general distribution, was based on the cow (*The Origin of Metallic Currency and Weight Standards* [Cambridge at the University Press, 1892], p. 133).

2. Burns, *op. cit.*, pp. 8-10.

3. Karl Polanyi, Conrad M. Arensberg, and Harry W. Pearson (eds.), *Trade and Market in the Early Empires* (New York: The Free Press and The Falcon's Wing Press, 1957).

4. The first to propose the theory that religion was the sole motivation for early coin types was Thomas Burgon of the British Museum ("Representations on Ancient Money," *Numismatic Journal*, Vol. 1 [1837]). Later this hypothesis was elaborated upon by Professor Ernst Curtius ("On the Religious Character of Greek Coins," translated by Barclay V. Head, *Numismatic Chronicle*, Vol. 10 [new ser.; 1870]). Additional study was done by Percy Gardner, whose *The Types of Greek Coins* (Cambridge at the University Press, 1883) contains many illustrations of the symbols of the deity on ancient coins.

Ridgeway (William Ridgeway, "The Origin of Jewelry," Report of meeting of the British Association for the Advancement of Science [1903], pp. 815-816.) contended that the types on coins were not of religious significance, but represented a previously existing barter unit. For example, the bull was the standard of wealth, and barter was conducted in terms of cattle; hence, when coins were produced, their value was indicated by placing the symbol of the bull upon them. These coin images, in other words, guaranteed that the weight and quality of the coinage stood at a parity with the object which it was customary to employ as a unit of bartering. The presence of tunny-fish on early coins would thus stem from the fact that the tunny-fish was a staple commodity, and hence was a bartering unit. Similarly, since double axes were used as units of barter, they were represented on coins. The ears of corn on the Metapontum coins were not a symbol of Demeter, according to Ridgeway, but were a symbol of a food used in bartering. The sun-tortoise, also found on early coins, was also a previously existing bartering unit, as was the Boeotian shield. The tendency to place religious types on Greek coins, Ridgeway said, was a later development.

5. Barclay V. Head, *Historia Numorum* (Oxford at the Clarendon Press, 1911), p. lvi.

One difficulty with the orthodox theory, according to George Macdonald (*Coin Types: Their Origin and Development* [Glasgow: James Maclehose & Sons, 1905], p. 19), is that many coins, particularly the early ones, have punning symbolism on their face which is difficult to interpret as having religious significance. For example, certain of the images contain punning devices which denote the name of a city, as in the case of the leaf of selinon (parsley) which is found on the coins of the city of Selinus.

However, Burgon regarded these punning symbols as religious in nature. Gardner saw in them a survival of the sacred legend by which the city obtained its name, rather than a play of wit, for the objects seemingly serving as puns were intimately associated with the religious cult.

Anthropology also tends to refute Macdonald's point of view, for word magic is very common among primitives; words, being confused with real objects, can be manipulated and used in incantations to bring about the fulfillment of wishes and to produce the same effect as the objects themselves. Freud's work on the nature of dreams and of wit indicates that punning is intimately related to the mechanisms of the *primary process*—the lower, less rational type of mental activity which is closely connected with the belief in magic. Gardner's suggestion is substantiated by the belief, held in numerous primitive cultures, that a certain sacred plant or animal is the ancestor of the group.

6. M. E. Babelon, *Les Origines de la Monnaie* (Paris: Librairie de Firmin-Didot, 1897).

7. George Macdonald, *The Evolution of Coinage* (Cambridge at the University Press, 1916).

8. Macdonald, *ibid.*

9. Curtius, *op. cit.*

10. Bernhard Laum, *Heiliges Geld* (Tübingen: Verlag von J.C.B. Mohr, 1924).

11. This etymology has been disputed.

12. In *A History of Greek Public Finance*, Vol. I, translated by Carroll N. Brown (Harvard University Press, 1933), pp. 210-11, A. M. Andreades commented on *Heiliges Geld* as follows: "Many errors in detail have been charged against it, and some violence is done to the archaeological data in order to fit them into the thesis maintained, a thing which frequently happens, however, when new and radical theories are formulated. One may be permitted to observe, also, that even if the hypothesis be regarded as correct, public finance even in the time of Homer had passed beyond this sacrificial stage, for the heroic kings had other revenues than the sacrificial victims.

"It is probable, however, that there is a measure of truth in the theory of Laum, and it is certain that the worship of the gods was up to the 6th and even the 5th century a most important factor in the expenditures and revenues of the small Greek cities."

13. A. Hingston Quiggin, *A Survey of Primitive Money* (London: Methuen & Co., Inc., Ltd., 1949), p. 283 (footnote).

14. Paul Einzig, *Primitive Money* (London: Eyre & Spottiswoode, 1949), pp. 379-386.

15. Bernhard Laum, *Das Eisengeld der Spartaner* (Braunsberg: Verlag der staatlichen Akademie, 1925).

16. Bernhard Laum, "Das Fischgeld von Olbia," *Frankfurter Münzzeitung*, Jhg. 18 (1918), ss. 439-50.

17. Cyril C. Richardson, "The Foundations of Christian Symbolism," *Religious Symbolism* (New York: The Institute for Religious and Social Studies, 1955), pp. 5-8.

Chapter eleven

1. Donald W. McConnell, Edith Ayres, A. Anton Friedrich, and Willard E. Atkins, *Economic Behavior* (revised ed.; Boston: Houghton Mifflin Company, 1939), p. 261.

2. George Frederick Kunz, *The Curious Lore of Precious Stones* (Philadelphia: J. B. Lippincott, 1913), p. 225.

3. William Ridgeway, "The Origin of Jewelry." Report of meeting of the British Association for the Advancement of Science (1903), pp. 815-816.

4. "Charms and Amulets (Roman)," Hastings *Encyclopedia of Religion and Ethics*, Vol. 3, p. 464.

5. G. Elliot Smith, *The Ancient Egyptians* (London: Harper, 1923), p. 205.

6. Paul Einzig, *Primitive Money* (London: Eyre & Spottiswoode, 1949), p. 216.

7. *Ibid.*, p. 223.

8. M. Berthelet, *Collections des anciens Alchimistes Grecs* (Paris: Georges Steinheil, 1888).

M. Berthelet, *Les Origines de l'Alchimie* (Paris: Georges Steinheil, 1885).

9. Franz Cumont, *Astrology and Religion among the Greeks and Romans* (New York: G. P. Putnam's Sons, 1912), pp. 36-7.

10. Jane Ellen Harrison, *Themis* (Cambridge at the University Press, 1927).

11. Henri Frankfort, *Kingship and the Gods* (The University of Chicago Press, 1948).

12. Ernst Curtius, *The History of Greece*, Vol. I (New York: Charles Scribner's Sons, 1902), p. 107.

Bernhard Laum, "Über die soziale Funktion der Münze. Eine Beitrag zur Soziologie des Geldes" (*Finanzarchiv*, Neue Folge, Bd. 13, Heft I), S. 122.

13. A. M. Hocart, "Money" in *The Life-Giving Myth and Other Essays* (London: Methuen & Co., Ltd., 1952), pp. 97-104.

14. Bernhard Laum, *Ueber das Wesen des Münzgeldes* (Halle A. D. Saale: Abteilung Verlag der Münzhandlung A. Riechmann & Co., 1929).

15. "Coins and Metals (Western)," Hastings *Encyclopedia of Religion and Ethics*, Vol. 3, p. 703b.

16. *Ibid.*, p. 592.

17. Ernest Jones, "The Symbolic Significance of Salt," in *Essays in Applied Psycho-Analysis*, Vol. II (London: Hogarth Press, 1951), p. 31.

18. Robert Means Lawrence, *The Magic of the Horse-Shoe* (New York: Houghton, Mifflin & Co., 1898), p. 168.

19. Karl Polanyi, Conrad M. Arensberg, and Harry W. Pearson (eds.), *Trade and Market in the Early Empires* (New York: The Free Press and The Falcon's Wing Press, 1957).

20. *The History of Herodotus,* Vol. I, translated by George Rawlinson (London: J. M. Dent & Sons Ltd., 1949), p. 50.

21. August Boeckh, *The Public Economy of Athens* (2nd ed.; London: John W. Parker, 1842 [translated by George Coernwall Lewis]), p. 235.

Gustav Glotz (*The Greek City* [London: Kegan Paul, 1929], p. 184, 245) gives further examples of this practice.

22. Gustav Glotz, *Ancient Greece at Work* (New York: Alfred A. Knopf, 1926), p. 230.

23. Bernhard Laum, *Heiliges Geld* (Tübingen: Verlag von J. C. B. Mohr, 1924), p. 115.

24. Laum, "Über die soziale Funktion der Münze," *op. cit.,* pp. 138-42.

25. Robert Shiells, *The Story of the Token* (New York: John Ireland, 1891), p. 29.

26. M. Rostowzew, *Römische Bleitesserae* (Leipzig: Dieterich'sche Verlagsbuchhandlung, 1905), pp. 14-16.

27. *Ibid.,* p. 22.

28. "Token," Hastings *Encyclopedia of Religion and Ethics,* Vol. 12, p. 357.

29. The origin of *tesserae* in cult symbols, and their relation to money have been remarked upon by Laum, *Ueber das Wesen des Münzgeldes,* p. 64 (footnote), and *Heiliges Geld,* p. 115.

30. The following discussion of méreaux and communion tokens is largely based on the article "Token," *op. cit.,* pp. 357-60.

31. The use of communion tokens in the United States is discussed by Mary McWhorter Tenney in *Communion Tokens* (Grand Rapids: Zondervan Publishing House, 1936).

32. Benjamin N. Nelson, *The Idea of Usury* (Princeton University Press, 1949).

Chapter twelve

1. Royden Keith Yerkes, *Sacrifice in Greek and Roman Religions and Early Judaism* (New York: Charles Scribner's Sons, 1952), p. 25.

2. Josiah Royce, "Loyalty and Insight" in *William James and Other Essays on the Philosophy of Life* (New York: The Macmillan Co., 1911).

Josiah Royce, *The Philosophy of Loyalty* (New York: The Macmillan Co., 1908).

3. Emile Durkheim, *Suicide,* translated by John A. Spaulding and George Simpson (New York: The Free Press, 1951).

4. Francis Macdonald Cornford, *From Religion to Philosophy* (London: Edward Arnold, 1912), p. 53.

5. Livio C. Stecchini is now preparing a work to be entitled *Introduction to Ancient Metrology*, which traces the relation between early metrology and the development of the mathematical conception of the universe. According to Stecchini, metrology first developed as "an attempt to assure justice in the contract of sale by mathematizing the relation" ("Why Study Metrology?," unpublished manuscript).

6. The epistemology in this book stems mainly from the thought of Edmund Husserl, particularly as expressed in his speech, "The Crisis of European Culture."

7. S. H. Butcher, *Some Aspects of the Greek Genius* (London: Macmillan & Co., 1916), p. 109.

8. James H. Oliver, *The Athenian Expounders of the Sacred and Ancestral Law* (Baltimore: Johns Hopkins Press, 1950).

9. Sigmund Freud, *Group Psychology and the Analysis of the Ego* (London: Hogarth Press, 1948), p. 80.

10. Roger Money-Kyrle, "Varieties of Group Formation," in *Psychoanalysis and the Social Sciences*, Vol. II (New York: International Universities Press, 1950), pp. 313-329.

11. Ian D. Suttie, *The Origins of Love and Hate* (London: Kegan Paul, 1948), p. 120.

12. Jane Ellen Harrison, *Themis*, (Cambridge at the University Press, 1927), p. 485.

13. Wilhelm Gerloff, *Die Entstehung des Geldes und die Anfänge des Geldwesens* (Frankfurt am Main: Vittorio Klostermann, 1947).

14. Bernhard Laum, *Die Geschlossene Wirtschaft* (Tübingen: Paul Siebeck, 1933). The conception we advocate is of course that of a universal community, rather than that of a narrow nationalism.

15. Stanley Edgar Hyman, "The Symbols of Folk Culture," in *Symbols and Values* (New York: Harper & Bros., 1954), pp. 307-14.

16. Wolfgang Köhler, *The Place of Value in a World of Facts* (New York: Liveright Publishing Corp., 1938), p. 34.

Chapter thirteen

1. Martin P. Nilsson, "Geschichte der Griechischen Religion," *Handbuch der Altertumswissenschaft*, Abt. 5, Teil 2, Bd. 1, S. 11.

2. Karl Abraham, "The Spending of Money in Anxiety States," *Selected Papers on Psychoanalysis* (London: Hogarth Press, 1927).

3. Jane Ellen Harrison, *Epilegomena to the Study of Greek Religion* (Cambridge at the University Press, 1921).

4. Emile Durkheim, *The Elementary Forms of the Religious Life* (New York: The Free Press, 1947).

5. J. J. Atkinson, *Primal Law* (London: Longmans, Green & Co., 1903).

6. J. C. Flügel, *The Psycho-Analytic Study of the Family* (London: Hogarth Press, 1948), pp. 131-132.

7. Francis Macdonald Cornford, *Principium Sapientiae* (Cambridge at the University Press, 1952), p. 253.

8. Jane Ellen Harrison, *Themis* (Cambridge at the University Press, 1927), p. 208.

9. *Totem and Tabu,* in *The Basic Writings of Sigmund Freud,* translated and edited by A. A. Brill (New York: The Modern Library, 1938), p. 923.

10. Warner Muensterberger, "Oral Trauma and Taboo," *Psychoanalysis and the Social Sciences,* Vol. II (New York: International Universities Press, 1950), p. 172.

11. For example, Freud's "Certain Neurotic Mechanisms in Jealousy, Paranoia, and Homosexuality" (*Collected Papers,* Vol. II [London: Hogarth Press, 1948], p. 239). Dr. Renato J. Almansi has discussed with me a patient who produced extensive material in which the bull is regarded as his father. This individual, who experienced unusually great excitement in watching bull fights, identified himself both with the toreador and the bull, each of whom he admired because of their courage and strength. Melanie Klein reports a patient's dream in which the bull represented both the father and mother. ("Mourning: Its Relation to Manic-Depressive States," *Contributions to Psycho-Analysis, 1921-45* [London: Hogarth Press, 1948], p. 332.)

12. Edward Lehman, "Feeding Problems of Psychogenic Origin. A Survey of the Literature," *The Psychoanalytic Study of the Child,* Vol. III-IV (New York: International Universities Press, 1949), p. 472.

13. Bertram D. Lewin, *The Psychoanalysis of Elation* (New York: Norton, 1950).

14. Sigmund Freud, "Mourning and Melancholia," *Collected Papers,* Vol. IV (London: Hogarth Press, 1948).

15. Sandor Rado, "The Problem of Melancholia," *International Journal of Psycho-Analysis,* Vol. 9 (1928).

16. Nilsson, *op. cit.,* p. 37.

17. Lewis Richard Farnell, *The Cults of the Greek States,* Vol. II (Oxford at the Clarendon Press, 1909), p. 434.

18. A. B. Cook, "Animal Worship in the Mycenaean Age," *Journal of Hellenic Studies,* 14 (1894), p. 158.

19. George Thomson, *Studies in Ancient Greek Society* (London: Lawrence & Wishart, 1949), p. 114.

20. Harrison, *Themis, op. cit.,* p. 128.

21. Margarete Bieber, *The History of the Greek and Roman Theater* (Princeton University Press, 1939), p. 22.

22. William Mitchell Ramsay, "Pisidian Wolf-Priests, Phrygian Goat-Priests, and the Old Ionian Tribes," *Journal of Hellenic Studies,* Vol. 40 (1920), pp. 197-202.

23. A. B. Cook, *Zeus,* Vol. I (Cambridge at the University Press, 1914), p. 441.

24. Lewis Richard Farnell, *The Cults of the Greek States*, Vol. I. (Oxford at the Clarendon Press, 1909), p. 100.

25. James G. Frazer, *Spirits of the Corn and of the Wild*, Vol. II (London: Macmillan & Co., 1925), p. 4.

26. John Ferguson McLennan, "The Worship of Animals and Plants," *Studies in Ancient History*, 2nd ser. (London: Macmillan & Co., 1896), pp. 491-569.

27. A. B. Cook, "Animal Worship in the Mycenaean Age," *Journal of Hellenic Studies*, 14 (1894), p. 168.

28. D. P. Costello, "Notes on the Athenian ΓΕΝΗ," *Journal of Hellenic Studies*, Vol. 58 (1938), p. 174.

29. Jean B. Cammann, *Numismatic Mythology* (New York: Wayte Raymond, Inc., 1936).

30. G. Pederson-Krag, "A Psychoanalytic Approach to Mass Production," *Psychoanalytic Quarterly*, Vol. 20, No. 3 (1951).

31. Geoffrey Gorer, *The American People* (New York: W. W. Norton & Co., 1948).

32. Edmund Bergler, *Money and Emotional Conflicts* (New York: Doubleday, 1951).

33. Albert Lauterbach, *Man, Motives, and Money* (Ithaca: Cornell University Press, 1954), pp. 138-44.

34. Agnes Baldwin, "Symbolism on Greek Coins," *American Journal of Numismatics*, 49 (1915), pp. 89-194.

Chapter fourteen

1. Karl Polanyi, Conrad M. Arensberg, and Harry W. Pearson (eds.); *Trade and Market in the Early Empires* (New York: The Free Press and The Falcon's Wing Press, 1957).

2. As was early shown by Bronislaw Malinowski in *Coral Gardens and Their Magic*, Vol. I (London: George Allen & Unwin Ltd., 1935), and *Argonauts of the Western Pacific* (London: G. Routledge & Sons, Ltd., 1922). Another well-known contributor is Meyer Fortes, who wrote *The Dynamics of Clanship among the Tallensi* (Oxford at the University Press, 1945) and *The Web of Kinship among the Tallensi* (Oxford at the University Press, 1949).

3. For a discussion of various theories of the origin of primitive money, see Paul Einzig, *Primitive Money* (London: Eyre & Spottiswoode, 1949). M. J. Herskovits summarized the anthropological literature on the origin of trading in *Economic Anthropology* (New York: Alfred A. Knopf, 1952). The possibility that trading originated in the gift exchange was discussed by Marcel Mauss in *The Gift*, translated by Ian Cunnison (London: Cohen & West, Ltd., 1954), as well as by Elizabeth Ellis Hoyt in *Primitive Trade* (London: Kegan Paul, 1926). Often these exchanges have a ceremonial character, as in the potlatch and the kula ring of the Melanesians.

A. M. Hocart suggested a theory of the religious origin of trading among the Fijians which is akin to Laum's. According to Hocart, the exchange of gifts in this culture took the form of an exchange of offerings to the gods of kinsmen in another clan. Frequently the offering was of the nature of a magical amulet. The original form of money was the fee paid to the priest who presided at the sacrifice. ("Money," in *The Life-Giving Myth and Other Essays* [London: Methuen & Co., Ltd., 1952], pp. 97-104.)

4. P. Huvelin, *Essai Historique sur le Droit des Marchés et des Foires* (Paris: A. Rousseau, 1897), p. 37.

5. T. F. G. Dexter, *The Pagan Origin of Fairs* (Cornwall, England: New Knowledge Press, 1930).

William Addison, *English Fairs and Markets* (London: B. T. Batsford, Ltd., 1953).

6. Hutton Webster, *Rest Days* (New York: The Macmillan Co., 1916), p. 122.

7. Huvelin, *op. cit.*, p. 122.

8. Bernhard Laum, *Heiliges Geld* (Tübingen: Verlag von J. C. B. Mohr, 1924), pp. 99-103.

9. Max Weber, *General Economic History* (Glencoe: The Free Press, 1950), p. 122.

10. J. P. Waltzing, *Étude Historique sur les Corporations Professionnelles,* Tome I (Louvain: Charles Peeters, 1895), p. 322. (My translation.)

11. Édouard Will, "De l'aspect éthique des origines grecques de la monnaie," *Revue Historique,* Fasc. IV, Oct.-Dec., 1954, pp. 209-231.

Polanyi, *et al.,* "Aristotle Discovers the Economy," *op. cit.*

12. Henry Sumner Maine, *Ancient Law* (New York: Henry Holt & Co., 1879).

13. Gustav Glotz, *Ancient Greece at Work* (New York: Alfred A. Knopf, 1926), p. 301.

14. Fustel de Coulanges, *The Ancient City,* translated by Willard Small (Boston: Lee and Shepard, 1874), p. 258.

15. Max Weber, *The Protestant Ethic and the Spirit of Capitalism,* translated by Talcott Parsons (London: George Allen & Unwin, Ltd., 1950).

16. Gilbert Murray, *Four Stages of Greek Religion* (New York: Columbia University Press, 1912).

17. Erich Fromm, *Escape from Freedom* (New York: Rinehart & Co., Inc., 1941).

INDEX